Muhammad

An Authentic Overview of His Life & Mission

MUSTAFA UMAR

Muhammad: An Authentic Overview of His Life & Mission

Copyright © 2013 by Mustafa Umar

All rights reserved. No part of this book may be reproduced or transmitted in any form or by any means without written permission of the author.

First Edition

Printed in the United States of America

ISBN-13: 978-1490991061

ISBN-10: 1490991069

www.mustafaumar.com

In the Name of God
The Most Kind and Merciful

CONTENTS

PREFACE	2
INTRODUCTION	6
THE NECESSITY OF AN ACCURATE PORTRAYAL	8
THE NEED FOR MUSLIMS TO KNOW THE PROPHET	10
METHODOLOGY	14
THE LIFE OF THE PROPHET AS A SEPARATE GENRE	18
PART ONE: BACKGROUND HISTORY	20
THE HOUSE OF ALLAH	22
THE AGE OF IGNORANCE	25
ARABIA	32
PART TWO: EARLY LIFE	34
THE QURAYSH	36
ORPHAN	37
SHEPHERD	39
A COALITION TO PROTECT THE WEAK	40
REPUTATION	41
MARRIAGE & FAMILY	42
REBUILDING THE KAʿBAH	43
SECLUSION	45
PART THREE: THE MISSION BEGINS	48
REVELATION	50
AN INFORMED OPINION	52
THE MESSAGE	53
THE SECRET CALL	54
PUBLIC DECLARATION	56
MASS REJECTION	58
PERSECUTION	61
ASYLUM IN ABYSSINIA	65
SOME RELIEF	68
POLITICAL TACTICS: BARGAINING AND PRESSURE	72
BOYCOTT & SANCTIONS	74

A Year of Sadness	75
Visit to Ṭā'if	79
Calling the Tribes of Arabia	81
The Pledges at ʿAqabah	83
Migration to Madīnah	85
Part Four: The Struggle to Survive	**90**
Arrival in Madīnah	92
Building the Mosque	94
True Brotherhood	96
Cold War	97
On the Brink of War	100
The Battle of Badr	102
Post-war Conduct	105
New Enemies	106
Treachery of the Qaynuqāʿ	110
The Battle of Uḥud	112
Preachers Murdered	116
Expulsion of Naḍīr	117
The Battle of the Trench against the Allies	118
Dealing with the Traitors of Qurayẓah	120
The Treaty of Ḥudaybiyah	121
Islam Spreads	124
The Siege of Khaybar	127
The Expedition of Mu'tah	129
The Conquest of Makkah	130
The Battles of Ḥunayn and aṭ-Ṭā'if	132
The Expedition of Tabūk	134
The Farewell Pilgrimage	137
The Prophet's Death	138
Epilogue	**140**
Appendix 1 – Early Sources	**142**

MUHAMMAD: AN AUTHENTIC OVERVIEW

Preface

I begin by praising Allah[1] and asking Him to bless the last messenger Muhammad[2] and all those who follow his example.

This book introduces the life of Muhammad, who was chosen by Allah to serve as the last vehicle through which the purpose behind human existence can be known. It is not enough only to believe in 'God' as the originator of this world and then neglect to inquire about the purpose of our very existence. Such a limited approach is referred to as 'deism' and is often the result of an oversimplified generalization that all religions must be manmade. According to Islam, prophets are sent by Allah to guide people. When the recipients of that guidance neglect or convolute it with interpolations or omissions, as has happened throughout history, another prophet is sent. In that sense, the resulting altered religion may correctly be described as manmade, although many elements of truth remain within. Muhammad was the last of these messengers sent by Allah and appeared at a time when the previous messages delivered by Abraham, Moses, Jesus, and all the other prophets had already been corrupted or lost.

The intention to write a book on the life of Muhammad arose the moment I picked up a few books on the subject. The

---

[1] Allah is the Arabic word for 'God' and will be used throughout the book, except when the context directly refers to a Jewish or Christian narrative.

[2] Muslims usually insert the words "peace be on him" after mentioning any prophet. We will omit this in writing for the sake of fluency. The same methodology has been followed by the great Imām Aḥmad ibn Ḥanbal [d. 241 A.H.].

literature was not to my taste, either because it was a poor English translation of a work written in a foreign language for a radically different audience or because the academically intense text didn't flow like the biographies I was used to reading. Much time passed before I could finally muster up the courage to write about so great a personality and so theologically sensitive a topic. Every time I began to compile notes, I recalled how unqualified I was for the task at hand. Furthermore, the alarming statement by the great scholar Ḥāfiẓ al-Dimyāṭī almost made me give up the idea entirely. He expressed his regret after writing a book on the life of the Prophet due to his overreliance on only a few sources. Later on, he realized that he had passed on many of the mistakes made by previous authors but his book had already been widely disseminated and those points could not be retracted.[3]

Nonetheless, it was nothing but the dearth of readable and reliable material which has compelled me to undertake such a venture. Both Muslims and non-Muslims alike have very few good resources on the life of the Prophet in English besides the biased works of orientalist and missionary professors. That is in addition to the more crafty compilations of sympathetic, but ignorant or agenda-driven, contemporary scholars. Whether the tone in these works is polemical or seemingly neutral, the poison of skewed ideas about the Prophet of Islam enters the body of the reader either way.

With few exceptions, the English works by Muslim authors are usually sloppy translations of antiquated or badly referenced books which were written for a particular audience in a

---

[3] Al-'Asqalānī, Ibn Ḥajar, *Fatḥ al-Bārī* (From *al-Maktabah al-Shamilah* [CD-ROM] 2.0) 12:126.

particular time. There is a pressing need for a work that is comprehensive, readable, authentic, and academic, all in one package. This endeavor is an attempt to achieve those lofty requirements.

I pray that Allah accepts this effort and counts the time I invested as being, at least somewhat, on par with the sacrifices made by people like Muṣʿab ibn ʿUmayr who initially introduced the Prophet to the people of Madīnah and then voluntarily used his body as a shield to protect the Messenger of Allah during the battle of Uḥud. It is a fact that Allah has only granted absolute perfection to His own book, the Qur'ān; therefore, my success in this endeavor lies only with Allah and I ask him to overlook my shortcomings and mistakes.

Mustafa Umar

Leicestershire. December, 2011

MUSTAFA UMAR

Introduction

MUSTAFA UMAR

The Necessity of an Accurate Portrayal

There has perhaps never been a more critical time for studying the life of the Prophet Muhammad. The amount of misinformation, coupled with a general ignorance, about Islam has led to much confusion and bias. So many people hear only a few tidbits about one or two incidents in the life of the Prophet and then make a decisive judgment concerning his character or the message of Islam that he brought. Such is the nature, and power, of false propaganda. To make things worse, the modern educated mind assumes that the ability to think critically is sufficient to make such judgments, regardless of whether all the facts are present or not. This perverted state of affairs is like that of an intelligent judge who passes verdicts based on his reason without pausing to weigh the available evidence in front of him.

Muhammad's life story actually represents the history of Islam in its final manifestation. How he received revelation, the persecution and difficulties he faced trying to propagate the message, and the eventual spread of Islam throughout Arabia and beyond are all part of that history. The life of the Prophet of Islam gives a picture of what Muhammad was really like. How did he behave in public and in private? What thoughts went through his mind? After receiving revelation from Allah, people responded to his message in several different ways. One group rejected him and labeled him an imposter. Another group considered him to be self-deluded and thus turned away from the message as well. The final group accepted him as a true prophet and followed the guidance he brought.

Today, many people classify themselves into a fourth category of apparent neutrality. They claim to reserve judgment concerning the prophethood of Muhammad and cannot make up their minds. Their hesitancy is rarely the result of timidity and usually arises out of an intellectual laziness or unconcern for things related to religion. One of these people might ask, "There are so many important persons in history and my time is limited; why do you insist that I investigate and make up my mind about Muhammad?" The answer is simple, yet multifaceted. Muhammad's claim to be the final messenger with the ultimate book of guidance from God is wholly unique from any other leader, philosopher, mystic, artist, etc. Whoever believes, or is willing to believe, that a 'Supreme Intelligence' not only created this world but communicated the purpose behind existence will find in Muhammad a conduit through which that message has been communicated. His life must be read without prejudice, and taking the facts as they are, rather than coloring them with the hue of another religious or philosophical paradigm.

If a reader is unwilling to take such a bold step then, at minimum, they can make up their mind about certain key questions regarding Muhammad: was he kind or cruel, what led him to engage in warfare, how was his message spread, how did he treat people who disagreed with him, etc.? Having unbiased answers to these questions not only determine an individual's attitude towards Islam but also affect the collective public opinion of a nation, which in turn could have such drastic consequences as massive genocide.[4]

---

[4] The Spanish inquisition and the more recent invasion of Bosnia by the Serbs are perfect examples of such terrorism, which requires a vast amount of Islamophobic propaganda to deceive the general population into supporting it.

The Need for Muslims to Know the Prophet

Muslims are in as much dire need of getting to know their Prophet as non-Muslims are. The following reasons are only some of the main benefits that can be accrued from such a study.

Proof of Prophethood

His life serves as a proof of his claim to prophethood. In order to be a Muslim in the true sense of the word, a person must be convinced that Muhammad was indeed what he claimed to be: a prophet sent by Allah. For that conviction to be firm and grounded it should transcend mere inherited beliefs and be based on knowledge. It is not a difficult task to believe Muhammad was indeed telling the truth after studying his life. His life story reveals that he had no ulterior motives for undergoing the difficulties he went through. His sincerity and character, coupled with the glaring clarity and consistency in the message that he brought, have convinced millions of people, even in the overly-skeptical secular Western society, to adopt the religion of Islam.

Role Model

He is an example for everyone who wants to follow in his footsteps. The Qur'an says: "Indeed, you have an excellent example in the Messenger of Allah".[5] Elsewhere, it speaks directly to the Prophet: "Indeed, you stand on an exalted standard of character."[6] Everyone needs a role model in their life. It is a human necessity. However, modern pop culture and marketing is ruthlessly indoctrinating Muslims, young and old, who are like empty cups under a waterfall, to adopt ethically

---

[5] Qur'an 33:21
[6] Qur'an 68:4

bankrupt entertainers as their role models. Even those Muslims who are more firmly grounded in knowledge and understand the concept of Islamic identity are still in danger and forced onto the defensive. Such a phenomenon of globalized pop culture is purely driven either by greed or cultural arrogance rather than a sincere desire to see others prosper. The best defense for a Muslim is to take the Prophet as a standard of what a role model should look like and Islam as a filter for determining what qualities deserve admiration in a person.

Sincere Love

Someone may have great love for a person without knowing them very well. However, that love is very shallow and can disappear when they learn more about the person. The love received by most celebrities and famous personalities has little grounding because their fans and followers know little about what they are truly like.

Muslims are instructed to love the Prophet more than anyone else in this world, including their own selves. In order to acquire a deep and grounded love for him, they must know what type of person he was and how much he cared for his followers [and even those who didn't follow him].

People are loved either for their own intrinsic qualities and behavior or for what benefits they give to others. From this perspective, the Prophet is loved by Muslims on both accounts. First, the fact that he was chosen by Allah means that his qualities and characteristics were attested to by the Creator of the Universe. Second, his teachings serve as a practical guide for how to please Allah, even several centuries after his demise. In fact, he was told in the Qur'an to declare to people: "Say, 'If you love Allah, follow me, and Allah will love you and forgive you your sins.'"[7]

A Balanced Picture

His life reveals a balanced picture of how the Messenger of Allah really was. There are many aspects of his life which are neglected by Muslims due to their ignorance, while other aspects are overemphasized without even realizing it. Scanning through a hundred, or even a thousand, reports about the Prophet by his companions will not give a full picture of the prophet if they are limited to only one aspect of his character and span only a few days of his life. A more holistic view is needed which is provided by a comprehensive history. Such a holistic view also reveals the strategic decisions that he made throughout his life. His mission of twenty three years underwent several stages and transitions: from keeping the message a secret to openly proclaiming it, from putting up with persecution to fighting back, etc. Each strategy had a context and provides an example of how to react when those circumstances present themselves again.

Contextualize the Sources of Islam

The life of the Prophet contextualizes the sources of Islam: the Qur'an and the Ḥadīth[8]. Without such a framework, isolated verses of the Qur'an or statements of the Prophet can easily be misinterpreted. There are many verses and teachings pertaining to beliefs, morals, parables, etc. which are crystal clear and don't require much context to understand. However, there are other verses and statements which must be understood

---

[7] Qur'an 3:31
[8] Ḥadīth refers to any statement or action of the Prophet. These *ḥadīth*s are compiled in books and serve as a primary textual source for knowing what the Prophet said and did.

through their historical background since they dealt with certain events during the life of the Prophet. In the absence of such historical information, these verses cannot be understood properly.

Take the verses teaching patience during persecution as an example. If the history about how the Muslims were persecuted is not kept in mind, there will be much loss in meaning. The Prophet was also accused by his enemies of being a poet. Without understanding the importance of poetry in Arabia, the challenge of eloquence that the Qur'an presented to the literary geniuses of the time, and the hostility of those who denied Muhammad's prophethood, it is quite difficult to understand why such an accusation would be made in the first place. A final example can be found in the battles which took place between the Muslims and their enemies. These wars have been mentioned by name in the Qur'an [e.g. Badr], and without background knowledge of these incidents, a reader of the Qur'an would be lost as to what is being referred to.

No book can be understood in a vacuum. However, many Muslims today fail to realize the importance of context due to their general ignorance of Islam. This has resulted in a very difficult and dangerous situation where the printed Islamic texts are in the hands, or in the pocket computers, of virtually everyone, Muslim or non-Muslim. A context must accompany the text if it is to be of any real benefit. Therefore, the life of the Prophet acts like a general introduction to Islam. This provides a framework in which to interpret any isolated incident and put it in its proper place.

Methodology

There have already been thousands of books written about the life of the Prophet Muhammad and this process will continue until the end of time. Each book serves a specific purpose. Therefore, no one should claim that there is no need for another fresh biography in English. The present work is based on several sources. While it does not claim to present any new groundbreaking research, there are several unique features that cause it to stand out from the rest.

Comprehensive Approach

This biography is confined to narrating the most significant events in the life of the Prophet without attention to unnecessary minute details such as the lineage of each individual, the history of various Arab tribes, excess geographical information, or anything else that would have little benefit for the average reader. Relating specific details of every incident in the Prophet's life would make the book too large for practical purposes.

Of course, it should be admitted that there must be a level of relativity in what constitutes a 'significant' event. Therefore, I have selected what I consider to be the most important events and details according to three criteria. First, priority has been given to events that the Qur'an has mentioned. If Allah chose to put an event in His book, then I deem it to be of the utmost importance. Second, the information and events selected by most of the Prophet's biographers has been given due consideration. Following this principle not only gives credit to scholars of the past but also creates a sense of cohesion within the Muslim community about what aspects of the Prophet's life people are familiar with. Third, incidents which teach the most relevant lessons for the average Western reader have been preferred over those that may be specific to certain individuals.

One of the reasons why we study history is to understand the present and build the future. This can only be accomplished if we focus on trying to extract lessons from the past rather than viewing them as mere events that have little significance in the practical sphere of life.

Precedence for Authenticity

This work attempts to be academically rigorous and give precedence to more authentic sources over less authentic ones. Historically, Muslim scholars did not strictly enforce such an approach when compiling biographies of the Prophet. The methodology implemented by those scholars can best be described in the statement of the great Imām Aḥmad ibn Ḥanbal regarding the most famous early biographer of the Prophet, Ibn Isḥāq: "We may report the life of the Prophet and other things from a man like Ibn Isḥāq. However, when we come to the lawful [ḥalāl] and prohibited [ḥarām], we need strong people like this [and he clenched his fist]."[9] His statement shows that a more lax criterion of authentication was employed in accepting historical events that did not affect the religion of Islam.

The reasoning is simple. A Muslim should not believe something about Allah based on a weak narration. Islam teaches what to believe about Allah, how to worship Him, and how to live a proper life. All these teachings are directly from Allah and cannot be mixed up with historical reports of dubious

---

[9] Al-Mizzī, *Tahdhīb al-Kamāl* (From *al-Maktabah al-Shamilah* [CD-ROM] 2.0), 24:422; al-Bayhaqī, *al-Asmā' wa al-Ṣifāt* (From *al-Maktabah al-Shamilah* [CD-ROM] 2.0), 2:420.

authenticity. However, if someone were to accept that some event occurred in a certain month, or a person was 40 years old, etc., it would not be detrimental to one's belief if that information turned out to be wrong.

This is precisely why Muslim scholars have been lenient in accepting historical reports but very strict in adopting something directly connected to Islamic beliefs or law. However, some authors were too lenient and included whatever stories they found interesting. In fact, one may often find a book which presents teachings not fully in line with the spirit of Islam, even in popular biographies of the Prophet. In the present work, we will follow the same methodology used by most scholars but will exercise more caution when utilizing historical sources, since bizarre or far-fetched stories can lead to much confusion in the minds of modern readers.

Indicate Causes behind Events

Many early biographers of the Prophet simply reported incidents in the Prophet's life with little or no analysis of those events. This may be praised as a very honest approach to history which reports the facts as they are, but it has also led to many misconceptions. For example, it is common to find several chapters in historical sources which say that the Prophet attacked such and such a city without mentioning why. Such an approach has led some modern historians who had no familiarity with Islamic Law to presume that no motive is required by Muslims to launch an attack. Books penned by Orientalists[10], on the other hand, went to the opposite extreme by attempting to read the minds of every person in history and

---

[10] An Orientalist is a Western scholar who studies Islam. The term is rarely used nowadays, probably due to Edward Said's criticism of the very term 'Orient' in his excusably critical book, *Orientalism*.

inventing bizarre motives which were not only mere conjecture but flew in the face of documented historical reports. This book will attempt to take a balanced approach and indicate causes and motives for events and decisions when they are sufficiently decipherable.

Highlight Lessons from the Past

Rather than just narrating stories, this work will highlight lessons behind each event. Such analysis will be built into the story itself. This approach follows the Qur'anic paradigm which narrates stories not merely to entertain but to teach lessons and morals. The lessons derived from each episode will be selected based on how relevant they are to contemporary circumstances.

The Life of the Prophet as a Separate Genre

Not long after the demise of the Prophet, his companions who were eyewitnesses established schools in which they would teach their students about Islam. Within those educational circles a distinct discipline eventually arose which studied the detailed life of the Prophet, from beginning to end. This subject came to be known as the Sīrah, which stood for the biography of the Prophet. There was another branch of knowledge called Ḥadīth which recorded the sayings and actions of the Prophet.

One would assume that there would be much overlap between the two, but it is not the case. The latter science consisted of individual incidents which usually highlighted a teaching of Islam. The books compiled in the field of Ḥadīth were usually organized according to subject matter such as beliefs, law, exegesis, etc. The science of Sīrah, on the other hand, was an attempt to present a chronological story about the life of the Prophet by giving preference to dates and major events, usually of a political or military nature.[11] As previously explained, the criteria of authenticity in each field differed greatly due to the nature of the content in each respective field. Almost any Ḥadīth could fall into the category of Sīrah, but not vice versa. Thus, these two fields generally emerged independently of each other.

---

[11] This is why many early biographers titled their books maghāzī, which means battles.

Part One: Background History

The House of Allah

The life of Muhammad begins in Arabia, but his story begins thousands of years before his birth. The book of Genesis, which both Jews and Christians consider to be a revelation from God, mentions the story of Abraham and his two sons, Ishmael and Isaac. Speaking about the firstborn child: "And as for Ishmael, I [God] have heard you: behold, I have blessed him, and will make him fruitful…and I will make him a great nation."[12] Later, it says: "God was with the boy as he grew up… and he lived in the Desert of Paran…"[13]

Paran is the area of Western Arabia[14] in which there was a valley named Bakkah.[15] This barren valley was surrounded by hills and completely uninhabited. Abraham was commanded by God to leave his wife Hagar and his son Ishmael there, all alone, as a test of their devotion. God caused a well to spring up for them and they survived in the barren desert.[16] Soon after, some of the surrounding tribes began to inhabit this valley, which became known as Makkah. Ishmael grew up with the Arab tribe of Jurhum, learned their language, and became known as Ismāʿīl.

Later, when Abraham, known in Arabic as Ibrāhīm, returned, he and his son were instructed by Allah to build a small place of worship dedicated to Him.[17] There were many temples and

---

[12] Genesis 17:20
[13] Genesis 21:20-21
[14] See Nomani, Shibli, *Siratun Nabi*, tr. Rafiq Abdur Rehman (Karachi: Darul Ishaat, 2003), 1:120-127.
[15] Psalms 84:4-6; for a discussion on how this reference has been misunderstood by some biblical scholars see Nomani, Shibli, *Siratun Nabi* 133-135.
[16] Genesis 21:17-19

shrines around the world where all sorts of idols were worshipped, but this was the first structure entirely dedicated to the worship of Allah alone[18], and was destined to be the last as well. It was a simple, rectangular building made of stone, a little taller than an average man, and was called the Ka'bah.

Ibrāhīm and his son invited the Arabs to only worship Allah and renounce all other false gods. This belief spread in Makkah and some surrounding regions. Then he was instructed to invite the surrounding tribes to visit the Ka'bah and worship there, an act known as the Pilgrimage [Ḥajj] since it requires a journey.[19] The Ka'bah became known as the House of Allah, and served as a place of worship for all the Arabs who accepted that only Allah deserves such devotion.

One way to worship Allah was by bowing or prostrating towards the Ka'bah. Since the building was both simple and empty, no one could think that they were worshipping a created object. Another way to worship was to walk around the building while praising Allah. By making the House of Allah the center point of one's motion, it implied that Allah was the central focus of their worship and thoughts.

Ibrāhīm made a special prayer to Allah that He should make this land safe and that his family should be protected from idolatry.[20] He knew, through years of experience with his own people, that the temptation for idolatry and immorality is extremely strong.

After his parents passed away, Ismā'īl remained in Makkah with his family. He eventually was chosen by Allah to become a

---

[17] Qur'an 22:26
[18] Qur'an 3:96
[19] Qur'an 22:27-28
[20] Qur'an 14:35

prophet like his father. He continued to instruct his people how to live life in accordance with Divine guidance and they followed him.

After Ismāʿīl, his descendants only worshipped Allah and followed the moral teachings that both father and son were inspired with. The Kaʿbah remained a place dedicated to worshipping Allah and believers would come from all over Arabia for the pilgrimage. Makkah became the spiritual capital of monotheism.

The Age of Ignorance

Idolatry

After several centuries, things had changed. The believing Arabs, through carelessness and neglect, gradually forgot the true way of Ismāʿīl and became lazy in following the guidance sent by Allah. Even their pilgrimage became more of a formulaic ritual than an act of worship. The first and most essential teaching of worshipping only Allah was all that remained, but even that was soon to be demolished.

Around the 4th century, the tribe of Khuzāʿah eventually managed to kick the descendants of Ismāʿīl out of Makkah and one of their chiefs introduced idol worship into the holy city.[21] He set up hand-carved statues in front of the Kaʿbah and people were encouraged to worship these man-made objects. Since most people had already forgotten the guidance sent by Allah they gradually turned to idol worship. Within a few centuries, idolatry prevailed around Arabia and the House of Allah had turned into a House of Idolatry. Nothing remained of the religion of Ismāʿīl but a few lifeless rituals and customs.

There were over three hundred idols both inside and around the Kaʿbah. When people would come for pilgrimage, they would take some stones from around the sacred area back home with them. In due time, these stones were also worshipped and became like portable idols that could be taken anywhere.

Idolatry became an addiction. One man who couldn't find a rock to worship piled together some dirt, poured some milk over it and began to walk around the heap of mud in the same way

---

[21] Bukhārī

pilgrims would walk around the Ka'bah to worship Allah.[22] Another equally creative man was once traveling through the desert and forgot to bring his idol along. He had some dates with him, so he fashioned an idol out of the dates and began to worship the fruit statue. Later on, he became hungry and ate his god.

What were such people thinking? It is not that they didn't believe in a Creator; they did.[23] However, they began to believe that Allah could not be approached directly and that these idols were the mediators between them and Allah.[24] They would bow down before these idols in worship and ask them to fulfill their wishes and protect them from danger. In order to appease these statues, they would even slaughter animals and dedicate the sacrifice to them.[25] Many even believed that the statues carved with their own hands actually possessed some type of special powers.

Idolatry became an organized religion with the invention of certain religious customs. It was declared that certain crops and animals must be dedicated for the idols. No one was allowed to eat them, and people donated generously.[26] Another innovated custom was that any sheep or camel which gave birth to ten female children in a row was deemed a sacred animal that no one was allowed to touch.[27]

There were other Arabs who didn't believe in Allah at all. Some were pure materialists who only believed that time eventually

---

[22] Bukhārī
[23] Qur'an 29:61, 43:9, 43:87
[24] Qur'an 10:18, 39:3
[25] Qur'an 5:3, 6:121
[26] Qur'an 6:136-138
[27] Qur'an 5:103, 6:139

destroys everything.[28] Others worshipped the sun, the moon, or certain stars and planets. Most of the idol worshippers had little or no concept of an afterlife.

The masses believed in all sorts of superstitions. While performing the pilgrimage instituted by Prophet Ibrāhīm, someone invented the idea that the Makkans who wanted to enter their houses must do so through the back door to avoid misfortune.[29] Many people believed that the soul of a murdered victim floats around in the form of an owl until it is avenged. Fortunetellers and astrologers were regularly sought for advice and for luck.[30] Featherless arrows were labeled and cast like dice in order to decide serious matters like whether to travel to a certain place, to marry a particular person, or even to wage war. These arrows, which were cast in the name of a certain idol, had even been used to determine who a child belonged to in the case of adultery.

Morals

The Arabs possessed a few excellent qualities. They were extremely generous and hospitable, going out of their way to take care of guests. Courage was a highly praised virtue, and they would fight till the death if they were convinced about an idea. The Arabs had a strong sense of loyalty, particularly to their family and tribe. They possessed a firm will and lived a simple life. But aside from these few noble traits, their morals were not much better than their beliefs.

Drinking and gambling were rampant. Compounded interest on loans, known as usury, was common. It made the rich even

---

[28] Qur'an 45:24.
[29] Qur'an 2:189
[30] Bukhārī

richer and exploited the poor. If the unfortunate fellow who took the loan could not pay it back, the interest would kick in, and now he owed even more. Even if he died, the debt would be transferred on to his family.

Women were generally looked at as inferior beings, unless they came from a noble family. When a child was born, parents would openly express their discontent if it was a girl.[31] The Arab mentality felt that a boy would grow up to earn money for the family and be able to fight in case of a war, whereas a woman could not. Some fathers would even bury the girl alive, out of fear of poverty, without any social censure.[32] A woman could never inherit, neither from her husband nor from her parents. A man was allowed as many wives as he wanted and women could never petition for any type of divorce.[33] Prostitution was common and became an accepted social norm. One way in which marriage took place was that a prostitute would put a flag on her house and allow any man a free visit. Later, when she became pregnant, she would call every client that visited her to decide which one of them the child looked like. Whomever she chose would take her as a wife and would not be allowed to refuse.[34]

Very few people could read or write, or had any type of formal education. The only science worth mentioning was poetry, of which the Arabs were masters. However, even their eloquence was misused since most of their poetry consisted of self-praise, depicting women as sex objects, and praising their own drunkenness. Illicit relationships had become so common that

---

[31] Qur'an 16:58-59
[32] Qur'an 6:151, 16:58-59, 17:31, 81:8
[33] Qur'an 4:22
[34] Bukhārī

even one famous Arab poet boasted about how he had committed adultery with his cousin, and these vulgar lines were hung on the Kaʿbah during the pilgrimage season for all to admire.

In order to make a living, four months of the year were deemed sacred, and fighting was strictly prohibited. This gave safe passage to the caravans traveling towards Yemen in the winter and Syria in the summer for trade. Nonetheless, over a petty issue, tribal wars would be fought for years, with several people slain in the process. Since there was no central government or code of laws, every extended family formed a tribe, composed of several smaller clans, and each tribe existed within their own space. The tribal pride usually overshadowed any sense of justice, since a man was expected to support his own family even if they were the offending party. It was in the interest of every clan and tribe to make as many alliances as possible in order to survive. This period of darkness in Arabia later became known as the 'Age of Ignorance', since the people were ignorant of any Divine guidance from Allah.

Other Religions

There were some Jewish communities a few hundred miles north of Makkah who had managed to spread Judaism in the southern region of Yemen and even rule the area for a while. However, when the Jewish king began persecuting the Yemeni Christians, the mighty Abyssinian Empire based in Ethiopia, with the aid of the Romans, managed to oust him from power. This resulted in a significant Christian presence in Yemen. Several Arab Christians also resided near the borders of the Romans, who were Christian. However, both Jews and Christians were unable to have any major impact on the prevailing idolatry of the Arabs in general.

In reality, it was not only Arabia but the whole world that was in the 'Age of Ignorance'. Judaism was marked by an overemphasis on formulaic rituals and outward piety while many Rabbis misused their authority and became corrupt. Deliberate alterations had crept into the books revealed to Prophet Mūsā [Moses] and racial superiority became a fundamental tenet of the religion. Christianity did not fare much better. The true teachings of ʿĪsā [Jesus] had become so corrupted that he began to be worshipped alongside Allah. The doctrine of salvation gave the green light for people to follow their base desires while believing they will be forgiven. The concept of Trinity was eventually adopted which was so complex and mysterious that people claimed to worship one God while picturing three different persons in their mind.

In Persia, people had special temples where they actually worshipped fire. Many Arabs in Yemen also adopted this religion after the Persians ousted the Christians here in the 6th century. However, outside the temple, people did whatever they wanted and had no fixed code of morals. Buddhism in India and Central Asia had become as idolatrous as Arabia with statues and shrines dedicated to the Buddha. Brahmanism in India was so idolatrous that their gods reached in the millions while people were divided into separate social classes based on their family background. The lowest group was eternally destined for slavery in order to serve the highest group, who were treated like gods.

The world was virtually in a state of chaos. The message brought by previous prophets like Ibrāhīm, Mūsā and ʿĪsā who were sent by Allah to reform mankind had become utterly corrupted. Men and women had forgotten Allah and couldn't tell the difference between right and wrong. But Allah had not forgotten his creation.

Arabia

Geography

Arabia is the largest peninsula on Earth, surrounded by water on three sides. It covers over a million square miles of desert. The region is sandy and mountainous, and therefore mostly unpopulated. There is a scarcity of water and the climate is very hot and dry. This is why most towns exist only where there are sources of water, while the wandering Bedouins are nomads who travel from place to place wherever a source of hydration is to be found. Such geographical features made it difficult, and unattractive, for any major empires to even consider conquering Arabia.

Political Situation

By the 6th century, the two major world powers were the Romans to the west of Arabia and the Persians to the east. The former was known as the Byzantine Empire and had colonized the lands of Egypt and Syria while the Sassanid Empire of the Persians had recently taken control of Yemen in the south. Nonetheless, most of Arabia had never experienced any foreign occupation and remained in quite a primitive state. In fact, the primitive nature of the Arabs is revealed in their language which had to borrow foreign words for such everyday terms associated with civilization such as coin, lantern, jar, cup, and basin. Since there was no central government or rule, it was a pretty dangerous place. Could there be any good expected to come out of such a primitive and backwards area?

Part Two: Early Life

The Quraysh

Around the 5th century, Quṣayy ibn Kilāb led a revolt against the tribe of Khuzāʿah and managed to retake control of Makkah. The members of his tribe, known as the Quraysh, were direct descendants of Prophet Ismāʿīl. By the 6th century, the Quraysh enjoyed a position of honor among the several tribes scattered around Arabia because they took care of the Ka'bah and the pilgrims that would come to visit. They would feed the visitors, give them shelter, and organize trade festivals where people could do business. Makkah was a magnet that attracted tribes from all over the peninsula to come for worship, even though it had now become a place of idolatry.

The tribe of Quraysh consisted of many different families, or clans. The family of Hāshim was now among the most prominent. ʿAbdul Muṭṭalib, the chief of the clan, became the unofficial leader of the Quraysh in Makkah. He had many children, but one of his favorite was ʿAbdullah. It was predicted that he would carry on the legacy of his father, but it was not to be. ʿAbdullah married Āminah from the Zuhrah clan. A few months later, on his way to Yathrib in the north, he became ill and passed away, leaving his wife pregnant.

Orphan

Āminah gave birth to a son on Monday[35] in the month of ar-Rabīʿ al-Awwal, in the year 570.[36] The child's grandfather named him Muhammad, which meant 'the praised one', a rare name in Arabia. It was the custom in Arabia that infants of noble families be brought up in the desert with the Bedouins. Some tribes had a reputation for nursing and raising children, like the Saʿd ibn Bakr, where Muhammad spent his childhood. There was less disease and the pure language was uncorrupted by urban living. A child would grow up to be tougher and there were less immoral influences than in the city. Muhammad grew up in the household of Ḥalīmah who was his foster mother and learnt the ways of the desert. He would visit Makkah every few months to see his mother, only to return to the desert again. Eventually, he was returned to his mother a few years later. Little Muhammad was from one of the noblest families among Quraysh.[37] Arabs preserved their family trees very carefully because it was an important consideration in their society, and Muhammad's lineage was well known through his 21st paternal grandfather, ʿAdnān, who was one of the prominent descendants of Ismāʾīl.[38]

After a short while, when Muhammad was only six, Āminah became very ill and passed away while mother and son were on a journey. Muhammad, now having lost both mother and father, was taken care of by his grandfather ʿAbdul Muttalib. He

---

[35] Muslim
[36] There is a discrepancy on whether the year was 570 or 571 and this is due to the discrepancy in converting from the lunar calendar to the solar Christian calendar, which has undergone many changes with dates being adjusted by certain monarchs.
[37] Muslim
[38] Bukhārī

treated him like his own son.[39] In fact, he allowed Muhammad to sit next to him on his special seat in front of the Ka'bah, a privilege which his own children did not even enjoy. However, when young Muhammad was only eight, he also passed away. It was his uncle Abū Ṭālib who would raise him from now on. Abū Ṭālib loved his nephew very much and would even take him along when he journeyed to Syria and other places for business.

---

[39] Ḥākim

Shepherd

However, Abū Tālib was not very wealthy like his father, so Muhammad had to work to earn a living and help his uncle. He began his career as a shepherd, taking care of flocks of sheep and goats for the people of Makkah.[40] A shepherd learns a great deal of responsibility. He must guide the sheep, together as a group, and protect them from predators at the same time. It also teaches the shepherd patience and gives him much time to think and reflect away from the excessive noise of the city. Many of the Prophets sent by Allah to other communities were known to be shepherds at some point in their life because a person's occupation has a great effect on his personality.

---

[40] Bukhārī

A Coalition to Protect the Weak

Due to the tribal nature of the society, people in power were able to get away with crimes against those in weaker positions. Once, a merchant from Yemen came to Makkah and was cheated by one of the noble men of Quraysh named al-'Āṣ ibn Wā'il. The man pleaded with the leaders in Makkah, but al-'Āṣ and his clan were too well connected. Finally, some influential men felt sorry for him and decided that something must be done. This event occurred shortly after a war that raged between the Quraysh and another tribe. Many people were tired of warfare, so a few leaders assembled together in the house of 'Abdullah ibn Jud'ān and formed a pact where each leader would stand up for the weak and oppressed, regardless of how powerful the oppressor may be. It was called 'The Pact of Excellence', or *Ḥilf al-Fuḍūl*. They went to the criminal and forced him to return the merchandise to the victim. Muhammad proudly took part in this pact and used to praise it throughout his life.[41]

---

[41] Aḥmad

Reputation

It was well known that Muhammad was one of the few who refused to worship idols from a very young age. He would visit the Ka'bah but direct his worship only to Allah. It was common practice to touch a certain idol while going around the Ka'bah and praying, but Muhammad used to skip this part. He also abstained from eating any meat that was slaughtered in the name of an idol.[42] However, he never openly protested against idol worship and mostly kept his beliefs to himself.

After shepherding for a few years, he took an interest in trade and became a businessman who would trade people's goods for them. Most noblemen among the Quraysh were merchants by profession. However, Muhammad stood out from the rest due to his honesty and sincerity. He quickly became known in Makkah as *al-Amīn*, 'the honest one'. Also, he was known for his high morals, chaste character, and avoidance of wine, gambling, illicit relationships, and other vices.

---

[42] Bukhārī

Marriage & Family

A wealthy lady named Khadījah hired him to trade her merchandise in Syria for her. He was to receive a percentage of commission from the deals. He performed the task with such precision and honesty that she later proposed to marry him by sending one of her friends to ask him if he was interested. She had received many proposals after her second husband had died, but she refused all of them. However, she saw something special in Muhammad and was taken by him.

Muhammad had to raise the needed money to pay for her dower which was about 500 dirhams. He was twenty five while Khadījah was not only quite older than him but she had been married twice before. This did not deter him though since she had all the qualities he could ask for: a righteous character, noble lineage, beauty, and wealth. Muhammad and Khadījah were married and eventually had six kids: two boys and four girls. Both boys died in their infancy while only one daughter outlived their father. Yet, the two boys were destined to be substituted by two others.

A young boy named Zayd ibn Ḥārithah was separated from his family and ended up in Makkah. Muhammad and Khadījah decided to adopt him and he became known as Zayd ibn Muhammad.[43] A few years later, there was a famine in Makkah and this proved to be very difficult, especially for Abū Ṭālib who had to support a large family. In order to ease the burden on him, Muhammad and Khadijah took one of his sons, 'Alī, into their household and raised him as their own child. Thus, they became a happy family of eight.

---

[43] Bukhārī; The word 'ibn' means 'son' and is commonly found in most Arab names to indicate lineage.

Rebuilding the Ka'bah

Around the time Muhammad was thirty five, the Quraysh faced a great challenge.[44] The Ka'bah was on the verge of collapsing. It had been damaged by major flooding and was desperately in need of repair. They finally decided to tear part of it down and rebuild it anew. It was agreed upon by the leaders that only pure money would be used, not wealth earned from usury, prostitution, or theft. They proceeded in their task and rebuilt the walls until it was time to put one of the special stones, known as the black stone, back in its place. This stone was special because it was the final stone to be placed by Prophet Ibrāhīm and was a marker for where pilgrims should start their worship.

Each tribe demanded that they should have the honor of replacing it back in its position. The arguing became so severe that war seemed imminent. One determined clan, the 'Abd ad-Dār brought a bowl filled with blood and had each family member dip their hands in it, signifying that they were willing to fight to the death. They allied with the 'Adī clan and refused to budge. There was a stalemate for several days and a war was about to break out. However, an elder among the Quraysh suggested that the next person who comes to visit the Ka'bah would decide who gets the honor, and everyone agreed.[45]

The Quraysh identified the man who was walking towards the Ka'bah and they shouted, "*Al-Amīn* [The Honest One]! It's Muhammad!" They were happy that it was someone they held in high esteem. If it was anyone else, he probably would choose his own clan for the honor. But instead of favoring his own

---

[44] Abd ar-Razzāq
[45] Aḥmad

family, Muhammad appeased all clans by asking for a sheet. He placed the black stone on it and had one leader from each clan hold a side of the sheet while they all carried the rock to its place. He then replaced the stone himself and the reconstruction was completed. War was averted through a policy of compromise.

However, the Quraysh ran out of clean money and shortened the dimensions of the Ka'bah, leaving it more cubic than rectangular. For the missing part, a low semicircular wall was put in the place of the original structure to mark the boundaries. They raised the walls higher than the original building was and placed a roof over it, to prevent thieves from entering. The Quraysh also raised the door of the Ka'bah several feet above ground level so they could control who would be allowed to enter.

Seclusion

Muhammad continued his profession as a merchant for many years and lived a simple life with his wife and children. He was disturbed by the immorality present in his society. But the most despicable of all the vices of his people was their idol worship. They paid lip service to Allah while they worshipped statues and pictures made with their own hands. He could see right through the façade of the dry rituals that the Arabs engaged in, even during the Pilgrimage.

In fact, he was not alone in his aversion to idol worship. There was Waraqah ibn Nawfal who had abandoned idolatry and become a Christian. He was able to read the scriptures of the Jews and Christians in Hebrew and decided to follow this path. It is unknown what form of Christianity he followed, but since he was a scholar, he probably had his own idea about what Prophet ʿĪsā [Jesus] really taught.

There was also Zayd ibn ʿAmr ibn Nufayl who went to Syria in search of a better religion. He met a Rabbi and was interested in becoming a Jew. After asking him some questions about Judaism he felt unhappy with what he learned about the religion. Then he met a Christian scholar and was interested in becoming a Christian. However, he was again displeased with the answers. He decided to simply worship Allah alone and he raised his hands to the sky, "Allah, I declare that I follow the religion of Ibrāhīm!"[46] Indeed, the way of Ibrāhīm had become virtually lost, and it was impossible to try to reconstruct or revive the original teachings with nothing short of another revelation from Allah. He used to stand in front of the Ka'bah and announce, "None of you really follows the way of Ibrāhīm

---

[46] Bukhārī

except me!"[47] Zayd was quite vocal about his beliefs and used to criticize people who sacrificed animals in the names of their idols.[48] He was also known to rescue the little girls who were about to be buried alive by their fathers. "Give her to me, I will bring her up," he pleaded. Once the girl would grow up, he would approach the parents, "Now, if you like, you can take her back. Or, if you prefer, I can continue to take care of her."[49]

But people like Waraqah and Zayd were few and far between, and there is no record of them ever trying to collectively change society. In fact, Zayd died while repeating the statement, "Allah, if only I knew how to worship you, I would have done so."

Muhammad was now about forty[50] and he began to go on retreats in the mountains around Makkah, spending a few weeks by himself. Rather than socializing and engaging in tribal politics, he preferred to be by himself. He had a wife and children to look after and worked full time, but these retreats became a priority in his life. One of his favorite destinations was a cave in Mount Ḥirā', about two miles from Makkah. The cave was very small and just big enough for one or two people to fit inside. He would take enough food and provisions with himself and stay in the cave, worshipping Allah and reflecting on life and its purpose. When his supplies ran out, he returned home. After a while, he felt the urge to go again to the mountains.[51] During this period he began to have dreams which would come true exactly as he saw them in his sleep, but he didn't know what that meant. This period of intermittent retreats continued for

---

[47] Bukhārī
[48] Bukhārī
[49] Bukhārī
[50] Bukhārī
[51] Bukhārī

several months on end. It was as if he was searching for something. He felt lost and was in need of guidance, just as much as anyone else.[52]

---

[52] Qur'an 93:7

MUHAMMAD: AN AUTHENTIC OVERVIEW

Part Three: The Mission Begins

Revelation

One night, near the end of the month of Ramadan[53], Muhammad was praying and meditating when he felt another presence in the cave.[54] "Read!", commanded a voice. "I cannot read," Muhammad responded honestly, for he was illiterate[55] like most Arabs. Something grabbed him and squeezed him so hard until he couldn't endure the pain anymore, then released him. "Read!", the voice demanded again. "I cannot read," responded Muhammad once more. It grabbed him a second time and clenched him. This was no dream. A mere pinch would have been sufficient to wake him up if it was. When he couldn't stand the pain anymore, he was let go. "Read!" Muhammad was frightened. What is this? What was happening? There were so many questions but no time to think. He had to respond quickly, "I cannot read." Again he was seized and crushed for the third time, then let go. The voice recited the following words:

> *"Read[56] in the name of your Lord who created. He created man from a clinging form. Read! Your Lord is most generous. He taught by means of the pen. He taught man what he did not know."[57]*

It was clear that he was being told to repeat what he had heard, and he complied fully. Those words were entirely etched in his memory. Then the presence left, and he was alone again.[58]

---

[53] Qur'an 2:185, 97:1
[54] Bukhārī
[55] Qur'an 29:48
[56] The Arabic word *iqra'* can mean 'read' or 'recite', depending on context.
[57] Qur'an 96:1-5
[58] Bukhārī

What just happened? What were those verses? Muhammad, being an Arab, was familiar with poetry, but this was neither poetry nor prose. There was no time to reflect. He was frightened and ran down the mountain. He went straight home to his wife, who could comfort him the most. "Cover me! Cover me!" Khadījah placed a blanket over him until he calmed down. Then he told her about his experience and admitted that he was scared. He recalled the verses to her, letter by letter. She immediately consoled him saying, "Allah will not disgrace you. You are kind to your family, you aid the weak, you help people in need, you are generous with your guests, and struggle for the truth." She firmly believed that Allah would not allow anything bad to happen to a righteous man.[59]

---

[59] Bukhārī

An Informed Opinion

Khadijah took him to her cousin Waraqah ibn Nawfal who now had become blind in his old age. Since he had become Christian and was well versed in the religion, he might offer some insight into what had happened. When he heard Muhammad's story he exclaimed, "I swear by Allah, you are the prophet of this community. The angel of revelation that came to Mūsā [Moses] has come to you." This was shocking news to Muhammad. A prophet of Allah? This was unheard of in Makkah since the time of Ismā'īl. But that was not the only shock. Waraqah continued, "If only I were younger and could live to see your people kick you out." Muhammad was shocked because he was well respected among his people. "They would kick me out?!" he responded. "Indeed. Everyone who came with this message was attacked by their people. If I live to see that day I will fully support you." But it was not to be. Waraqah died soon afterwards, but now it was clear to Muhammad that he was the Messenger of Allah.[60]

---

[60] Bukhārī

The Message

The first revelation received in the cave indicated that the Prophet was going to be taught certain things directly from his Creator. This served to reestablish the connection between Allah and man, which had once been open to previous prophets. Then, other verses were inspired to him commanding him to pray throughout the night. The reason given was specifically that he would soon be entrusted with a difficult mission.[61] Prayer would help him to build up the strength he needed to fulfill that mission.

Soon afterwards, that mission was clarified in a subsequent revelation. Muhammad was the Messenger of Allah who must call people to worship only Allah and abandon all other deities.[62] From now on, he would not be isolating himself in prayer anymore but warning others as well. Religion would no longer be seen as something personal where people kept their beliefs to themselves. The task would not be an easy one, but it had to be done.

---

[61] Qur'an 73:1-6
[62] Qur'an 74:1-5

The Secret Call

The Messenger initially only confided in those people he knew could be trusted. Makkah was the heart of idolatry and it would not be easy to change things overnight. The mission required long-term planning and thus began with a secret call to only those who would likely be interested.

The Prophet began with his own household. After the meeting with Waraqah, Khadījah was already convinced that her husband was indeed a Prophet. She knew her husband in and out for the last fifteen years and it was crystal clear to her that he was neither a liar nor possessed. She was thus considered the first believer. Then his cousin Ali and his adopted son Zayd followed suit. They were both young adults and could tell the difference between an imposter and a truthful man. Young people sometimes have the ability to see things that even experienced elders are unable to perceive.

The first man outside the family to accept the message was Abu Bakr. He had been the Prophet's best friend for many years. He was a merchant of noble lineage and was respected throughout Makkah for being both a philanthropist as well as an expert genealogist. Abu Bakr immediately began to tell his close associates about the Prophet. Quite a few responded such as ʿUthmān, al-Zubayr, ʿAbd al-Raḥmān, Saʿd and Ṭalḥah. The message was beginning to spread in Makkah, albeit covertly.

This religion was called Islam, meaning submission and surrender [to Allah]. The people who followed Islam were named Muslims [i.e. those who submit and surrender]. The nascent Muslim community would meet and pray secretly, to avoid causing a stir in Makkah. Whenever a new revelation came down, the Prophet would teach it to some of his followers. They would memorize the verses and act upon them. The early revelations consisted of short, but powerful and eloquent, reminders concerning the oneness of Allah, the reality of prophethood and warnings about the Day of Judgment[63]. The revelation was known as the Qur'an. It referred to itself as a book, although it had not been compiled into a finalized written form as we understand a book to be. The revelation was to continue for several years and guide the Prophet through his mission.

Abu Bakr urged the Prophet, "let's call people to Islam publicly." But the Prophet refused, "we are too few." Nonetheless, most people in Makkah were hearing whispers here and there about the Prophet and his 'new religion'.

---

[63] This refers to the notion that all people will be resurrected after their death and held accountable before Allah in the next life.

Public Declaration

A few years passed and the Messenger of Allah continued to secretly invite people to Islam. By the third year of his prophethood there were no more than fifty believers. Then the revelation to declare the message publicly came:

> *Now openly proclaim what you are commanded and turn away from the idolaters. Indeed We will suffice you against the mockers.*[64]
>
> *...and warn your own tribe.*[65]

The Prophet understood what had to be done. He ascended a hill in Makkah where urgent announcements were made. "People of Quraysh!" he called out. The influential people came to listen to the urgent alert. "Would you believe me if I told you there is an enemy behind the hill ready to attack the city?" he asked. "Of course," they replied, "you are not a liar." He put forward this statement, not only to test them, but to serve as an analogy. What he was about to tell them required them to acknowledge a principle: the Prophet, standing on the hill can see something in front of them, due to his elevated position, that they are unable to perceive. If they accept his testimony, they can prepare themselves to fight the coming army and save themselves from destruction. However, if they doubt him, or try to verify the information, there would be no time to prepare, if he was telling the truth. The test, therefore, lay in whether or not they were prepared to take him on his word without asking for empirical evidence. They had answered in the affirmative, for they knew his character and reputation.

---

[64] Qur'an 15:94-95
[65] Qur'an 26:214

Then the Messenger of Allah called each clan by name and declared, "I have been commanded by Allah to warn you and I cannot protect you in this world. Nor can I promise you anything in the next world unless you acknowledge and submit to the worship of Allah alone." Everyone was stunned and remained quiet until his uncle, Abu Lahab, broke the silence: "May you be destroyed! You called us here for this?!" His uncle was primarily interested in business and acquiring wealth. A pause to reflect on the purpose of life was, for him, nothing but a waste of time. Abu Lahab's position among the Quraysh was one of great influence and his reaction led the people to follow him when he left in protest.[66]

It was clear this minor setback should not deter the Messenger of Allah from his mission. Someone who rejects something today may accept it tomorrow. The Quraysh had not even seriously considered the message or reflected on what it entails. How could they reject it so quickly? The Prophet began to go around Makkah and call people to Islam, both individually as well as in their public gatherings. During this period, several verses describing how previous prophets like Nūḥ [Noah], Ibrāhīm [Abraham], Yūsuf [Joseph], Yūnus [Jonah], Mūsā [Moses] and ʿĪsā [Jesus] called their people towards worshipping Allah. These verses also indicated the opposition these prophets faced from their people, implying that the Prophet must be prepared to have patience in his mission. Not only did he speak to his people but he began to pray openly at the Kaʿbah where everyone gathers for worship. Thus, his prayers and recitation of the Qur'an at the House of Allah became another way to convey the message to others, while worshipping Allah himself.

Mass Rejection

The Prophet continued his preaching despite the negative reactions from the majority of Makkans. When people have lived their life in one way for such a long time, it is not easy for them to change. There were several different reasons why people refused to accept the message of Islam. Most of them were so attached to their tribal customs that they could not imagine abandoning the ways of their ancestors. Whatever their family or tribe considered to be good was good. How could idol worship be such a bad thing when their wise elders practiced it? Some people were very attached to their idols and were afraid that if they stop worshipping them, something bad might happen. Out of fear, they remained in their idolatry. The leaders among the Quraysh were fearful of losing their position of power. If they followed this Prophet while the rest of the Arabs remained in their idol worship, they would not only lose their prestige but their business as well, since the annual pilgrimage to the Ka'bah created a prosperous economy. Finally, people are naturally afraid of changing their lifestyle. The Arabs loved their freedom to indulge in all types of immoral behavior and to follow this Prophet would mean that they would have to live a clean and moral life. For them, the teachings of Islam seemed like inconvenient shackles that only served to strip away their freedom to do whatever they felt like at the moment.

The Makkans not only rejected the message but they fought against it. Their opposition began in the form of insults and accusations. Some people began to openly mock the Messenger of Allah: "Couldn't Allah find anyone else besides you?"[67] While the Prophet had a noble lineage and excellent character, he was

---

[66] Bukhārī, Muslim
[67] Qur'an 43:31

lacking in wealth and political clout. Many Arabs believed that the status of a person is determined by their wealth and political power in society. Some resulted to character assassination, calling the Prophet a magician[68], a poet or insane[69]. They didn't know how to explain the verses of the Qur'an that emanated from his lips. These few words had such a great impact on the listeners that it required some type of explanation as to how Muhammad got such messages. Others set challenges to the Prophet to bring this or that miracle. Yet another reason was clan rivalry. Hāshim, the Prophet's clan, was in constant competition with the clan of Umayyah and Makhzūm for honor and power. To accept that Hāshim had received the gift of prophethood is something they could never rival, or accept. This is why much of the hostility came from both these clans, particularly Umayyah.

Now the Pilgrimage season was around the corner where Arabs from all over the peninsula would come to Makkah. Now that the call to Islam was public, would the Prophet be left to spread his message to other tribes as well? The leaders of the Quraysh could not allow this to happen. They gathered together and decided that they would need to come up with one specific accusation against the Prophet to tell the visiting pilgrims. Everyone from Makkah must be on the same page so no one can doubt their integrity. First, they thought of calling him a fortuneteller, but the idea was rejected because his message didn't resemble the style that those practitioners employ. Someone insisted, "Let's call him insane; he is a man possessed." However, that idea was also discarded since he doesn't show any signs of insanity or possession. Another man

---

[68] Qur'an 38:4
[69] Qur'an 15:6, 68:51

insinuated, "Why not call him a poet?" This idea would not work either because the verses of the Qur'an don't resemble any type of poetry and have no meter. They finally agreed on calling him a sorcerer that has the ability to break up families and turn son against father, despite the fact that they knew he didn't resemble someone who engages in these black arts. Nonetheless, it would instill the most fear in the consumers of such propaganda and they would likely be too afraid to give his message even a thought. They sent their delegates to the edges of Makkah to inform everyone who came to Makkah before they even entered the city.

Persecution

Islam was making progress, slowly but surely, despite the negative propaganda. People began to make fun of the believers openly, laughing at them as they walked by.[70] So the Quraysh stepped up their persecution and began torturing several Muslims, especially the slaves and poor ones. Being a tribal society, those with little or no connections were open targets.

Bilal, a black slave from Ethiopia who had accepted Islam, was dragged out into the burning hot desert by his owner, Umayyah ibn Khalaf, and forced to lie with his back on the scorching sand. Then, a giant boulder was placed on his chest and he was told, "You will stay like this until you die or until you reject Muhammad and worship our idols." He would respond by saying, "One! One!" meaning that he will only worship Allah alone. One day, during the torture process, Abu Bakr passed by, purchased Bilal, and set him free, as he did with six other Muslim slaves who were being persecuted.

Khabbāb was another unfortunate slave to be tortured. His owner would force him to lie down on burning hot coals while someone stood on top of him. He had burn marks all over his back for the rest of his life. One day, sick of the torture, he complained to the Prophet, "Why don't you pray for us?!" The Prophets face turned red and he responded, "People in the past would have their flesh torn apart with iron rakes, but they never abandoned their religion. Don't worry, Allah will establish this religion and make peace in the land...but you people are too hasty."[71]

---

[70] Qur'an 83:29-33
[71] Bukhārī

ʿAmmār ibn Yāsir was not even a slave, but his family was not from the original inhabitants of Makkah and therefore lacked connections. Both his parents, Yāsir and Sumayyah, had also accepted Islam, and were all tortured together. One day the Prophet passed by them, unable to do anything, and said, "Have patience and you will have paradise." Sumayyah took the statement to heart and remained as firm as a rock. While being tortured by one of the inveterate enemies of Islam, Abu Jahl, she was stabbed with a spear and died, making her the first martyr in Islam. ʿAmmār, on the other hand, succumbed to the pressure. In a moment of weakness, while being tortured, he rejected Islam and pledged his loyalty to the idols. His tongue contradicted what was really in his heart. So he went to the Prophet and told him what had happened. The Prophet consoled him and explained that true belief lies in the heart. The verses were revealed:

> *"With the exception of those who are forced to say they do not believe, although their hearts remain firm in faith, those who reject God after believing in Him and open their hearts to disbelief will have the wrath of God upon them and a grievous punishment awaiting them."*[72]

The verses made it clear that as long as ʿAmmār still believed in his heart, that false confession will not count against him in the sight of Allah.

Abū Dharr did not live in Makkah but heard about the new prophet. He was a man inclined towards worshipping only Allah so he needed to find out more. He sent his brother to Makkah to get more details but was not satisfied with what he had heard. Finally, he decided to go and investigate the issue

---

[72] Qur'an 16:106

himself. As soon as he reached Makkah, he immediately realized that he had to be careful whom he talked to. He lived for several days next to the Kaʿbah, drinking nothing but the water provided for visitors. Eventually, he managed to meet ʿAlī who covertly led him to the Prophet. "Follow me, but if you see me bend down to fix my shoes, take it as a sign that someone is following us and leave immediately," cautioned ʿAlī. As soon as Abū Dharr met the Prophet and learned what Islam was all about, he accepted.

The Prophet advised him, "Abu Dharr, keep your Islam secret and go back home. When you hear that we are victorious, come back." But Abu Dharr, in his excessive zeal, responded, "I swear by Allah, I will announce my Islam publicly in front of everyone." He went straight to the Kaʿbah and publicly announced that he had become Muslim. Immediately some of the Quraysh jumped on him and started beating him like a punching bag. The Prophet's uncle ʿAbbās, who had not yet accepted Islam, intervened and warned the people, "You better watch out! You don't want to kill a man from the tribe of Ghifār!" The people instantly stopped because they knew that their merchandise must pass through this area on the way to Syria. If they severed relations with the Ghifār, it would only hurt their business. Abū Dharr barely made it out alive, but his enthusiasm only grew stronger. The next day, he returned and announced his Islam again. A new group this time pounced on him and ʿAbbās had to intervene again. Abu Dharr had fulfilled his desire to let his acceptance of Islam be known, so he returned back home.

With such persecution, many Muslims preferred to keep their Islam a secret, even from their own parents. Such a feat was often difficult, because there were spies everywhere just waiting to expose another follower of the Messenger of Allah to the Quraysh.

Asylum in Abyssinia

The persecution began slowly but gradually increased over time. Even many noble Muslims with clan ties were being targeted. In the fifth year of prophethood, the Messenger of Allah recommended that some of the believers migrate to Abyssinia. This land, which is across the Red Sea in Africa, was run by a just king known as the Negus [*Al-Najjāshī*]. Over a dozen Muslims, both men and women, migrated, even the Prophet's own daughter, Ruqayyah, with her husband Uthmān. However, the furious Quraysh sent two envoys, Abdullah ibn Abi Rabi'ah and 'Amr ibn al-'As to try to secure their extradition through bribery and misinformation.

They began by presenting special gifts from Makkah to the advisory council of the king. Then they addressed the Negus:

> *"Some young fools have sought refuge in your kingdom. They left the religion of their people, but they didn't enter your religion either. They have come with a fabricated religion, which neither of us recognizes. The noblemen among their people have sent us to you to return them home. They are their parents, uncles, and family members and know better what to do with them."*

The advisors of the king agreed and told the king that he should send the Muslims back. The Negus became furious and responded that he would not extradite someone who sought asylum in his kingdom without hearing them out. So he called them and asked them to explain themselves. Ja'far, a nephew of the Prophet, got up and spoke:

> *"Dear king. We were an ignorant people. We worshipped idols and ate the meat of dead animals. We were used to lewd behavior, breaking family ties and harming neighbors. The strong among us oppressed the weak. That is how we lived, until God sent a*

messenger to us, whose nobility and honesty we had been fully aware of. He called us to worship the only God and give up our inherited worship of statues and idols. He told us to speak the truth, fulfill promises, keep family relations and be kind to neighbors. He forbade us from evil, bloodshed, shamelessness, lies, and deceit. He told us to stop the misappropriation of the property of orphans and avoid false accusations. He told us to pray, give charity, and fast. We believed in him and acted on his teachings. So we worshipped only God and no one else, we forbade what was forbidden to us and made lawful what was made lawful to us. This is why our people turned against us, tortured us and tried to make us return to worshipping idols instead of God and consider lawful the indecencies we used to do. So when they oppressed us and we couldn't take it anymore we sought protection in your land. We chose you over others hoping that we would be safe here and not oppressed."

The king asked Ja'far, "Do you have any of these verses with you that are supposed to be from God?"

"Indeed," replied Ja'far. The king wanted to hear the Qur'an, so Ja'far wisely selected some passages from the chapter titled Maryam [Mary], who was the mother of Jesus. He knew the king was a devoted Christian, so he recited:

Mention in the Qur'an the story of Mary. She withdrew from her family to a place in the east and secluded herself away; We sent Our Spirit to appear before her in the form of a perfected man. She said, 'I seek the Lord of Mercy's protection against you: if you have any fear of Him [do not approach]!' but he said, 'I am but a Messenger from your Lord, [come] to announce to you the gift of a pure son.' She said, 'How can I have a son when no man has touched me? I have not been unchaste,' and he said, 'This is what your Lord said: "It is easy for Me— We shall make him a sign to all people, a blessing from Us."'[73]

---

[73] Qur'an 19:16-21

The king and the court bishops who were present were so moved that they began to cry. The Negus then regained his composure and said, "These verses and what was given to Jesus are two rays emanating from the same light. He then turned to the two Makkan envoys and told them that he would never extradite the Muslims. They were free to stay and worship in Abyssinia for as long as they wished.

It seemed like the Quraysh had failed, but the envoys would not give up so easily. ʿAmr came to the Negus the next day and said, "Did you know that they insult Jesus by calling him a slave?" The king was taken aback. Had he been so easily deceived by these Muslims? The matter required an investigation. The Muslims were summoned again and asked, "What do you say about Jesus, the son of Mary?" Jaʿfar took on the position of spokesman once again and responded, "We only say what our Prophet taught us. Jesus is the servant of God and His messenger. He is His word and spirit that He inspired to the Virgin Mary." The Negus bent down and picked up a small stick from the floor and said, "By God, Jesus did not say anything more than the length of this stick than what you have said." The king returned all the gifts to the two envoys and sent them home. The Muslims were granted asylum and the envoys returned to Makkah unsuccessful. On hearing the good news, more Muslims migrated, and their number reached around a hundred in Abyssinia where they lived for several years. Many noble Muslims migrated as well, to live in peace and security.

Some Relief

It was difficult to keep calling people without results, but the Prophet had to persist. One day, in the sixth year of the mission, Abu Jahl verbally abused the Prophet and insulted him. He was one of the worst enemies of Islam and did his best to stop the message, but the Prophet did not respond to his insults and went home. Ḥamzah, one of the uncles of the Prophet, was returning from a hunting expedition. He was a soldier by nature and was known for his bravery and strength. As soon as he approached the Kaʿbah, a woman who had overheard what happened notified him of the incident concerning his nephew. He went straight to Abu Jahl and hit him over the head with his longbow. Then he said, "You dare insult him while I'm with his religion? I say what he says. C'mon, hit me back!" Abu Jahl decided to close the issue. It is unknown whether Hamzah's reaction at the time was out of tribal pride to protect his nephew or a genuine acceptance of Islam. Nonetheless, soon afterwards, it was clear that his heart had changed and he sincerely accepted Islam and changed his ways. His acceptance of Islam came as a great shock to Makkah. Ḥamzah's Islam proved to be a great source of strength for the Muslims and would help ease the persecution.

With most companions in Abyssinia, the Muslims in Makkah were badly in need of some more relief. Seeing that Hamzah's addition to the Muslim community only served to strengthen Islam, the Prophet prayed, "Allah, strengthen Islam with whichever of the two is more beloved to you: Abū Jahl or ʿUmar ibn al-Khaṭṭāb." Both these men were staunch enemies of Islam and regularly used to persecute the weaker Muslims. Abu Jahl was crafty and had much political clout while ʿUmar was tough and feared throughout Makkah. Both men seemed to be lost causes. One Muslim had even remarked, "It is more likely that al-Khaṭṭāb's [ʿUmar's father] donkey would accept Islam before ʿUmar would." But only Allah knows what is in a person's heart.

ʿUmar was known to be a heavy drinker and used to engage with his friends in drinking competitions. One night, he went out looking for some friends to get drunk with, but couldn't find anyone. Instead, he decided to go to the Kaʿbah and worship the idols. When he reached the sanctuary, he overheard the Prophet praying and reciting Qur'ān. He hid himself and continued to listen. "These are definitely the words of a poet," he thought to himself. Right at that moment the Prophet recited the verses, "This is the speech of an honored messenger, not the words of a poet – how little do you believe!"[74] ʿUmar was shocked. He then said to himself, "This must be a..." but before he could even finish his thought the Prophet recited, "Nor is it the words of a soothsayer – how little do you reflect! This is a message sent down from the Lord of the Worlds."[75] ʿUmar was now dumbfounded, for that is exactly the excuse he was going to make. This incident softened his heart for a moment towards Islam and probably was his first step towards ever considering it seriously.

But ʿUmar's anger soon made him forget whatever temporary reflection he might have had. He continued his hobby of torturing innocent Muslims until one day, he decided to put an end to this matter once and for all. Nuʿaym was a man who had managed to keep his Islam a secret. He happened to be walking down the street one day when he spotted ʿUmar carrying his sword in a fit of rage. "Where are you headed, ʿUmar?" asked

---

[74] Qur'an 69:40-41
[75] Qur'an 69:42-43

Nuʿaym. "To kill Muhammad and put an end to this nonsense," he responded furiously. He was shocked because he knew that ʿUmar wasn't joking. He tried to think of a way to protect the Prophet. No one else seriously considered killing the Prophet because it would mean that they would wage war on the entire clan of Hāshim and its allies. But ʿUmar was a man who was so determined that his own life didn't matter, once he had made up his mind to do something. "Why don't you take care of your own family first?" responded Nuʿaym. "What do you mean?" retorted ʿUmar. Nuʿaym would never deliberately put the life of another Muslim in danger. But he thought to himself that the safety and security of the Messenger of Allah takes precedence over everything. "Your sister and her husband have become Muslims." ʿUmar immediately changed his destination and went straight to his sister's house.

Fāṭimah and her husband Saʿīd had managed to keep their Islam a secret, knowing that ʿUmar would persecute them if he were to find out. ʿUmar heard the two of them reciting Qur'an from outside and barged into the house and began to beat Saʿīd to a pulp. His wife interfered and tried to help her husband only to receive a strong blow from the infuriated ʿUmar across the cheek. "Yes, we're Muslim, so do whatever you want!" she exclaimed. It was only when ʿUmar saw the blood on his sister's face that he began to feel some remorse. "Let me see what you were reading," inquired ʿUmar. Fāṭimah had managed to hide the paper from which the Qur'an was being read before the intruder had entered. After some hesitation, she gave it to him. ʿUmar was one of the few people in Makkah who were literate. As he began to read his mood changed for the positive and he remarked, "This is excellent!" This was the first time ʿUmar had actually attempted to understand the message of Islam with his mental shields down. He was immediately convinced and wanted to declare his Islam in front of the Prophet. Fāṭimah could see that something had changed in her brother, so she told them where the Prophet was and he declared his Islam that very day.

He did not keep his Islam a secret. He went to the enemies of Islam and told them one by one that he had become a Muslim. They were enraged but there was nothing they could do, because they feared ʿUmar. Because of both Ḥamzah and ʿUmar, the Muslims were able to worship openly at the Kaʿbah without the Quraysh being able to do anything about it.

Bargaining and Pressure

Seeing that neither ridicule nor persecution seemed to stop the spread of Islam, the Quraysh attempted another strategy. They figured that they could win the Prophet over through negotiations and/or bribery. However, their idea of negotiating meant that sometimes Allah will be worshipped and other times the idols would be worshipped, so it seemed like a win-win situation. To such a preposterous idea the verses were revealed:

> *Say [Prophet], 'Disbelievers: I do not worship what you worship, you do not worship what I worship, I will never worship what you worship, you will never worship what I worship: you have your religion and I have mine.*[76]

The revelation made it crystal clear that there could never be any compromise in the fundamental principles of Islam. The essence of the Islamic message is to only worship Allah and abandon all other deities. Even a slight violation of this essential tenet would lead to a wholesale negation of Islam.

With negotiations supposedly out of the picture, the Quraysh resorted to pressure tactics. Abū Ṭālib, despite his refusal to accept Islam, was constantly defending his nephew's right to propagate his message. As leader of the Hāshim clan, he was a respected chief among the Quraysh and prevented anyone from touching the Messenger of Allah. The other chiefs of Quraysh knew what had to be done. They went to Abū Ṭālib and told him that his nephew is insulting their gods, mocking their religion, and revolting against their culture. They ordered him that he must stop protecting Muhammad, or suffer the consequences. Abū Ṭālib went to the Prophet and said, "My nephew. Your

---
[76] Qur'an 109:1-6

people came to me complaining. So make things easy on both of us, and don't overburden an old man beyond his capacity." The Prophet responded, with full confidence, "My dear uncle. I swear by Allah, if the people of Makkah bribed me by giving me the sun in my right hand and the moon in my left, I would not give up this mission." Overwhelmed with emotion, tears began to roll down the Prophet's cheeks. Abū Tālib, moved by his determination, responded, "My nephew, say what you want to say. I swear by Allah, I will not give you up for anything."

Boycott & Sanctions

The Quraysh were getting frustrated. They had tried every possible way to stop the message of Islam. But the more they tried, the more Islam continued to spread. Something more drastic had to be done. Some particularly Islamophobic leaders of the Quraysh held a secret meeting in which they decided to boycott the clan of Hāshim until they agree to hand the Prophet over to them. Not everyone was in favor of such drastic action, but the loudest and most stubborn voices managed to silence the others. An agreement was signed that both the clan of Hāshim and their close allies, the Muṭṭalib clan, would be boycotted by the Quraysh. No one would be allowed to buy, sell or intermarry with them.

Despite the fact that many members of the clan had not accepted Islam, their allegiance to the decisions of the clan took precedence and they put up with the sanctions. Times became tough and many people went without food and water for days, as if they had been hit by a famine. Food had to be smuggled in secretly by some good intentioned humanitarians of Makkah. Despite the difficult circumstances, the Prophet persisted in calling people to Islam. The situation lasted for three years until some of the Makkans decided that it was enough. Five men came together and formed an advocacy group to challenge the unjust boycott. They managed to effectively have the document cancelled after three long years of oppression.

A Year of Sadness

The ban may have been lifted but now Abu Tālib was ill and nearing his last days. Within a few months, he was overtaken by a chronic illness. His situation deteriorated and he was confined to bed. Before he breathed his last, the Prophet would try one last time to get him to reconsider Islam. He entered his room and pleaded, "My dear uncle. At least say that there is no god besides Allah, so that I can bear testimony for you in front of Allah." Before Abu Tālib could even consider the idea, two influential men from Quraysh were also present in the room and responded, "Abu Talib, would you abandon the religion of your father?" Abu Tālib had to weigh the pros and cons of such an important decision. If he accepted Islam, he would lose the honor and respect of both his clan and tribe. Furthermore, he would probably be accused of making such a hasty decision because of his fear of death. But if he rejected, his name would live on as a great chief among the Quraysh who remained loyal to his family and tribe. Abu Talib made his decision: he would stay on the religion of his forefathers.

The Prophet was grieved but he responded, "I will keep asking Allah to forgive you until I am forbidden to do so." Soon afterwards, the verses were revealed:

> *"It is not fitting for the Prophet and the believers to ask forgiveness for the idolaters – even if they are related to them..."[77]*

> *You [Prophet] cannot guide everyone you love to the truth; it is Allah who guides whoever He will: He knows best those who will follow guidance.[78]*

---

[77] Qur'an 9:113
[78] Qur'an 28:56

The revelations made it clear that Allah does not approve of anyone asking forgiveness for someone who died in a state of disbelief. Allah has given every person the freedom to choose whether to accept or reject the message. The decisions that people make are part of the test of life. If the Prophet were able to bypass the decision of someone he loved, like his uncle, the exam would serve no purpose.

Only a few months later, the Prophet lost his beloved wife Khadījah as well. He later remarked about how much he missed her company, "She believed in me when people disbelieved. She accepted me as truthful when people called me a liar. She even aided me with her own wealth."[79] Since Khadījah was the first one to believe in the Prophet, perhaps even before he believed in himself, she was given the good news of paradise before she died.[80]

The demise of Abū Ṭālib had immediate outward consequences for both the Prophet and the mission. His hostile uncle Abū Lahab took this opportunity to target his nephew. He forced his own two sons to divorce their wives, both of whom were the daughters of the Prophet. Even Abū Lahab's wife partook in the persecution by scattering thorns in the pathway that the Prophet was likely to walk through. Things became difficult, and this time the Prophet had no wife to find comfort in.

On one occasion, Abu Jahl was sitting with some of his friends near the Kaʿbah when he spotted the Prophet praying. "I dare one of you to get the guts of a camel and throw it on Muhammad when he goes into prostration," said Abu Jahl. ʿUqbah ibn Abī Muʿayt took on the challenge and went to fetch

---

[79] Aḥmad
[80] Bukhārī

the filth. He returned just in time to catch the Prophet going into prostration. Without hesitating, ʿUqbah emptied an entire container filled with the intestines of a camel onto the Prophet's back. Abū Jahl and his buddies burst into laughter. One of the Prophet's companions, Ibn Masʿūd was watching but could do nothing. The Prophet remained in prostration, continuing his prayer, until his daughter Fāṭimah came and cleaned the filth off his back. Only on this occasion the Prophet raised his voice and prayed against them, "Allah! Destroy Abu Jahl, ʿUqbah and everyone like them!"[81]

Another incident occurred again at the Kaʿbah. While the Prophet was praying, this same ʿUqbah wrapped a sheet around the Prophet's neck and began to strangle him. The Prophet was caught off guard and couldn't breathe. Abu Bakr happened to be nearby and rushed to the seen. He pushed ʿUqbah away from the Messenger of Allah and shouted, "Would you kill a man just for worshipping Allah!?"

It became open season to target the Prophet, now that his clan protection was virtually gone. It became a common experience for the Prophet to find his neighbors dumping their trash right in front of his house. People would interrupt him while he was reciting the Qur'an by shouting and yelling. Another man even childishly threw a handful of dirt on his head. Fāṭimah began to cry when she saw this, to which he responded, "Don't worry my daughter. Allah will protect your father." The Prophet was informed by Allah that his mission would eventually succeed, but he didn't know when. Seeing such persecution, even a respected man like Abu Bakr decided that it was time to migrate to Abyssinia. However, while he was on his way out of Makkah,

---

[81] Bukhārī

a well-respected chief decided to grant him full tribal protection, and he remained. But one thing was clear: Makkah seemed like a lost cause. It was now time to look for another place which could accommodate the continuation of the mission.

Visit to Ṭā'if

After ten years of spreading Islam in Makkah, the Prophet traveled to a nearby town called al-Ṭā'if, about fifty miles to the east. He visited the leaders from the tribe of Thaqīf, only to be insulted and rejected by them. Accompanied by his adopted son Zayd, they stayed in al-Ṭā'if for several days calling the people to Islam, but with little success. It seems that the leaders of Thaqīf still had some insults left to unleash on the Prophet. They incited the scum of society to throw stones at the Messenger of Allah and chase him out of the city. They targeted their legs to slow them down, but Zayd was even hit once in the head. After being chased out of the city they decided to stop and rest for a while because their legs were bleeding. The Prophet later remarked that this was the worst day he ever experienced in his life. But Allah was not to leave him without comfort. An angel appeared before the Prophet and told him that he could destroy the entire city because of what they did to him. But the Messenger of Allah refused saying, "I hope that Allah might make their descendants worship only Him."[82] The Prophet was not interested in personal revenge, only with conveying the message. It was enough comfort that Allah had sent an angel to inform him that His help was always near.

On the way back to Makkah, the Prophet faced a dilemma. The news must have already reached the Quraysh that he tried to seek refuge in al-Ṭā'if, but without success. Thus he would not safely be able to reenter Makkah unless he had tribal protection. He sent a message before entering the city to several influential people, but they politely refused. Finally, Muṭ'im ibn 'Adī offered him protection and he returned to

---

[82] Bukhārī

Makkah. The Prophet would never forget this kind gesture from a noble man like Mut'im.[83]

Soon afterwards, the Prophet was encouraged to remarry. He agreed to the idea and married Sawdah, an early convert to Islam. She had migrated to Abyssinia with her husband but had returned to Makkah after her husband had died. She was quite old and a little heavy, but the Prophet didn't mind because she had a cheerful personality. One day she prayed with the Prophet who, as usual, spent so long in his bowing that she held her nose out of fear that it might start bleeding. When she told the Prophet what had happened, they both had a good laugh about it. The Prophet now had an intimate companion as well as a woman to take care of the household.

---

[83] Bukhārī

Calling the Tribes of Arabia

For several years, the Prophet called the different tribes of Arabia to Islam during the pilgrimage season. Since most of the tribes would have at least some of its members go to Makkah every year, most of Arabia had already at least heard about the message of Islam. Whenever the Prophet would try to approach a tribe, Abu Lahab would follow him from behind and yell insulting remarks at the Prophet.[84] But this did not deter him from fulfilling his mission. A few individuals had accepted Islam from the various tribes but not one leader had responded to the call.

Once, accompanied by Abu Bakr, the Prophet went to the tribe of Zuhl. Abu Bakr asked, "Have you heard about the Prophet? He's right here, you can meet him." One man turned to the Prophet and asked, "O brother of Quraysh. What do you teach?" The Prophet responded, "That Allah is one and that I am His Messenger." Then he recited the verses:

> *"Say, 'Come! I will tell you what your Lord has really forbidden you. Do not ascribe anything as a partner to Him; be good to your parents; do not kill your children in fear of poverty'— We will provide for you and for them—' stay well away from committing obscenities, whether openly or in secret; do not take the life Allah has made sacred, except by right. This is what He commands you to do: perhaps you will use your reason.'"*[85]

The leaders of the tribe were present and were impressed by the message. But after brief reflection, they responded, "We cannot take a hasty decision to abandon our ancestral religion. Besides, we have an alliance with Kisrā [Chosroes, the ruler of

---

[84] Ḥākim
[85] Qur'an 6:151

Persia] and pledged that we will not ally with anyone else." The Prophet appreciated their frankness and responded, "Allah will help His religion."

The Prophet also had met the tribe of ʿĀmir and explained the message. One seemingly interested individual, Firās, responded, "If we support you and you are victorious over your opponents, will we be put in power after you?" The Prophet responded, "Everything is in the hands of Allah." The man retorted, "You expect us to put our lives in danger against all the Arabs and then give authority to someone else afterwards? We are not interested."

In the eleventh year of prophethood, a few men from the tribe of Khazraj accepted Islam. They lived in a town called Yathrib which had recently been plagued with constant civil wars. The recent Buʿāth war between the tribes of Aws and Khazraj had wiped out many of their fighting men, and they were in desperate need of a solution. Calamities tend to soften the hearts of even the most obstinate of people. This might have been one of the many reasons that interested them in Islam. Another reason was that there were several Jewish tribes living around Yathrib who often spoke about the coming of a new Prophet who would be victorious over his enemies. It was clear to them that this was definitely the man who matched the description and they would be better off accepting him before anyone else. Despite their acceptance, it would have to be seen whether others from the Aws and Khazraj were interested in the message of Islam as well.

The Pledges at ʿAqabah

The following year, the men from Yathirb returned with a delegation of twelve people to Makkah. The Prophet met them secretly at night at a place called ʿAqabah. This time, the Prophet made them take a pledge of loyalty: "you will not ascribe any partners to Allah, you will not steal, you will not commit adultery, you will not kill your children, you will not slander others and you will not disobey me in any good that I order you." The men, one by one, stretched their hands out and shook the Prophet's hand, signifying that they accepted the pledge.

Before they returned home, the Prophet decided to send Muṣʿab ibn ʿUmayr to Yathrib to teach Islam. Muṣʿab was one of the early converts to Islam and faced many difficulties. He was a young man accustomed to luxury because his family was very wealthy. But the moment he accepted Islam, his family disowned him and he had to migrate to Abyssinia. The Prophet had seen him go from riches to rags, all for the sake of Allah. He knew that Muṣʿab was the right person for the job.

As soon as Muṣʿab arrived, he began calling people to Islam and teaching Muslims about their new way of life. One day, while he was sitting with some Muslims instructing them, an important clan leader approached the gathering with a spear in his hand. It was clear from the look on his face that he wasn't coming to welcome the Muslims. "Stop deceiving the fools in our community with your new religion and get out of here!" he yelled. It was clear that he had received second hand misinformation about what Islam really was. Muṣʿab calmly and confidently responded, "Why don't you take a seat? If you like what we say, you can accept it. If you dislike it, then we'll stop bothering you." The man thought about it for a moment and decided that it seemed like a fair offer. The moment he heard what Islam truly was and listened to some verses from the Qur'an, he immediately accepted it. Muṣʿab continued to employ this non-confrontational technique for an entire year until virtually every household in Yathrib had at least one member of their family accept Islam.

It was now the thirteenth year of prophethood and this time seventy three men and two women went to Makkah to meet the Prophet during the pilgrimage season. They met again secretly at ʿAqabah, but this time they specifically requested that the Prophet come to Yathrib and serve as their new leader. Before accepting their offer, he took a pledge from each one of them: "you will listen and obey me whether it is easy or difficult, you will donate whether you are well-off or otherwise, you will encourage others to good and warn against the bad, you will not fear any censure when you do something for the sake of Allah and you will protect me the way you would protect your own families." It was clear that this pact involved much more than just performing deeds of personal piety. There was even a hint that they might have to defend against a physical attack from the Quraysh. But their faith was strong and they were prepared to face any difficulty that might come along. All of them accepted the pledge and they returned to Yathrib where Islam continued to spread even more.

Migration to Madīnah

The Prophet gave the green light for believers to start migrating to Yathrib, which was renamed to Madīnatun Nabī, meaning, city of the Prophet, or just Madīnah for short. As if the journey wasn't difficult enough, the Quraysh tried to stop as many Muslims from leaving as they could.

Ṣuhayb was once such example. He was originally from Persia but was captured and sold into slavery in Rome. He grew up there and learnt the language until he was later sold again in Makkah. The benevolent man who purchased him eventually set him free and he was known in Makkah as al-Rūmī, or 'the Roman'. He occupied himself with business and became quite wealthy. Nonetheless, since he was still viewed as a foreigner with no tribal connections, he was treated as a second class citizen. Since he was also one of the early converts to Islam, his status was even lower. It was time for Ṣuhayb to migrate to Madīnah. But just when he was on his way out, some of the Quraysh spotted him. "Where do you think you're going?! You came to Makkah as a slave and you think we're gonna let you leave with all that money?!" someone shouted. Ṣuhayb thought for a moment and immediately realized that he had no care for all that wealth. Being with the Muslims in Madīnah was a priceless journey. He gave up all his wealth just so that he could migrate. When the Prophet later heard about this transaction he remarked, "Ṣuhayb made a really good profit," referring to the reward he will get from Allah for such a sacrifice.

Another instance of the difficulty in migrating is in the story of ʿUmar, ʿAyyāsh, and Hishām. All three agreed to meet at a certain place in the morning so that they could travel together. Morning came, but Hishām was missing. He had been detained by the Quraysh but ʿUmar and ʿAyyāsh decided that they must continue according to plan. Just as they were leaving, Abu Jahl caught up with them and told ʿAyyāsh that he has a very important message for him. "When your mother heard you were leaving, she took an oath to stand in the sun and never comb her hair, until she sees you," said Abu Jahl. There was another man with him and he confirmed the news. ʿUmar warned ʿAyyāsh that it's a trick but they had already hit a soft spot in his heart. ʿAyyāsh was determined to go see his mother so ʿUmar traded camels with him and said, "This is a fast camel. Stay in the back and if you see anything suspicious you can speed away." The three men set off back towards Makkah on two camels. On the way, Abu Jahl started complaining about how slow his camel was. It was starting to slow down the entire group so he asked ʿAyyash, "do you mind if I ride on your camel?" Occupied with the thoughts of his mother's situation, ʿAyyash agreed. As soon as he knelt his camel on the ground the two men jumped on him and tied his hands. ʿAyyāsh was taken prisoner along with Hishām and it was only several months later that the Muslims managed to bust them out.[86]

Within two months almost all the Muslims had already migrated, while the Prophet himself remained behind with only a few of his companions. The Quraysh were furious that the Muslims had not only found asylum but were given charge over an entire city. Not only that but this city was on the way to Syria, which the Quraysh caravans would pass through in order to do business. This means that they would have to pass through Muslim territory in order to continue their business ventures to the north which usually amounted to about a quarter million gold dinars annually. Something had to be done.

---

[86] Bukhārī

The leaders of Quraysh held an emergency meeting with only one item on the agenda: how to stop Muhammad.[87] Various ideas were proposed but it was finally decided that they must kill him once and for all. But who would dare to kill him and wage war with the entire Hāshim clan and their allies? It had to be Abu Jahl who came up with the solution to their dilemma. He argued, "If we get one man from each clan to stab him exactly at the same moment, the blood would be on the hands of every clan. They couldn't possibly wage war against everyone, so they would settle for monetary compensation." The idea was ingenious, although not everyone was for it. Nonetheless, it was adopted at the end of the meeting.

The assassins gathered outside the house of the Prophet just before dawn, knowing that he usually goes to the Kaʿbah early in the morning. But the Prophet had already been informed about the plot and approached Abu Bakr the day before, "I have been given permission to migrate." "Will I have the honor of joining you?" responded Abu Bakr. "Yes," he replied. Abu Bakr had been preparing for the journey months in advance. He had two fast camels that were being fed with a special plant to make them even stronger.[88] Just before dawn, the Prophet slipped past the assassins undetected, with the help of Allah. He immediately headed to the house of Abu Bakr who had prepared everything for the journey. Everything was going according to plan. They immediately headed south, on foot, and hid inside a cave at the top of Mount Thawr. The cave was quite a few miles away from Makkah and in the opposite direction of Madinah because they knew that search parties would be looking along those routes. As expected, the Quraysh

---

[87] Qur'an 8:30
[88] Bukhārī

dispatched bounty hunters to pursue them, and offered a large sum of 100 camels for anyone who finds Muhammad, dead or alive.

They spent three nights in the cave while Abu Bakr's son would visit them every day to give them the news about what the Quraysh were up to. To avoid being detected, Abu Bakr had arranged for a shepherd to graze his animals on the way to mount Thawr to cover up the tracks in the sand.[89] While most bounty hunters were searching the roads to the north, one group of them decided to go south towards the mountain. They managed to make their way up the mountain and near the entrance to the cave. Abu Bakr heard their footsteps from inside the cave and became frightened, "If they just look down, they will see us." He was not afraid for himself but for the Prophet and the message of Islam. "Be quiet. We may be two, but Allah is the third," whispered the Prophet, meaning that Allah would protect them.[90] After searching around for a while, the men went away.

On the fourth day, they received news that the search effort was dying down so they moved to the next phase of the plan. An expert desert guide named Abdullah was hired by Abu Bakr. Even though he was not a Muslim, he could still be trusted even in these delicate circumstances. He arrived at the mountain with Abu Bakr's two special camels and enough food for the journey. They set out for Madīnah using a rarely used route through the scorching desert. They travelled by night to avoid being detected. Whenever they encountered any desert people who inquired who they were, Abu Bakr responded, "I am Abu

---

[89] Bukhārī
[90] Bukhārī; Qur'an 9:40

Bakr and this man is my guide." In order to avoid lying outright, although such a dangerous situation would have demanded it, he spun the word to mean that the Prophet was his guide in life.[91] Finally, after several days of travelling through the desert, Madīnah was in sight. The mission of Islam had entered a new phase. Muslims would no longer be a persecuted minority and they would have the freedom to practice Islam as well as structure society as Allah deemed fit.

---

[91] Bukhārī

Part Four: The Struggle to Survive

Arrival in Madīnah

The people of Madīnah had heard the news that the Prophet had migrated and was on his way. While they eagerly anticipated his arrival, there probably was a sense of worry in their hearts. The desert was a dangerous place and the Quraysh had many allies along the route to the North which they might use to harm the Messenger of Allah. When the time for his arrival drew near, the people of Madīnah would go out every day and stare in the horizon to see if their new leader would appear. Finally, after much delay, someone shouted from the top of a palm tree, "There he is!"[92] The people of Madinah were both overjoyed and relieved at the same time.

The first place the Prophet stopped at was a little village called Qubā'. It was an elevated settlement about three miles from Madīnah. Most of the migrants initially halted here after their journey. The messenger of Allah was given a warm welcome and stayed there for two weeks.[93] Even though they were exhausted from the journey, the Prophet immediately made plans to build the first mosque where Muslims could gather and pray.[94] He participated in the construction by carrying heavy stones with his own bare hands, setting an example for all future leaders.

After the mosque was complete, he headed towards the city. The people of Madīnah came out in crowds to meet him. The men wore their armor and carried their weapons, as was the custom in Arabia to show power, while many women were standing on the roofs of their houses singing songs and beating tambourines. It was the happiest day that Madīnah had ever

---

[92] Bukhārī
[93] Bukhārī
[94] Qur'an 9:108

witnessed and perhaps made up for the harsh treatment the Prophet received in Ṭā'if. It was the month of al-Rabīʿ al-Awwal, thirteen years after the Prophet received the first revelation from Allah. This migration marked a new phase in the mission of the Prophet and later became the point at which Muslims would begin their calendar.

Many people had never seen the Prophet before but only heard about him. Some people accidentally went up to Abu Bakr, who was still with the Prophet, and began to greet him instead. It was only when Abu Bakr shaded the Messenger of Allah as a sign of respect that they realized their mistake.[95] Everyone was keen on showing hospitality to the Prophet so they began to insist that he stay with them. The Messenger of Allah did not want to insult anyone so he decided to stay with his distant maternal uncles who lived in Madīnah, a fair gesture that would be understood by everyone.[96]

---

[95] Bukhārī
[96] Muslim

Building the Mosque

Again, the first task which the Prophet performed was to build a mosque where all believers could assemble and perform their prayers. A piece of land was purchased from two orphans, who offered to give it for free, but the Prophet insisted to pay them. Construction began almost immediately and everyone, including the Prophet, participated in its construction. The Muslims were singing songs and enjoying themselves while working for the sake of Allah. This mosque became known as "the mosque of the Prophet", but was merely a courtyard surrounded by mud walls and covered with palm tree branches. Eventually, some pebbles were spread on the ground to prevent the floor from becoming muddy when it rained.

In Makkah, the Muslims were not able to pray together in congregation because of the danger they faced. Now that that threat disappeared, the five daily prayers were prayed in a group in the mosque. Bilal, the former slave, was selected to have the honor of calling people to each prayer. Every time his voice cried out, "Allah is great!" people would stop whatever they were doing and would come to the mosque for prayer. A mosque is much more than merely a place of performing prayer. It is a shelter whereby those overcome by the anxieties of this world can escape and return to Allah, even if momentarily. Furthermore, the mosque is the center of society where people can meet each other, learn about Islam and even conduct important meetings.

In one corner of the mosque there was a platform called "Ṣuffah' which was covered with a roof. It was designated as a refuge for the homeless Muslims who did not have anywhere else to stay. These people would be sent food by the more fortunate Muslims and were often invited to their houses for meals. The numbers of these people, who became known as the 'people of the platform', were always in flux. They devoted their nights to prayer and their days to learning more about Islam. The Prophet encouraged some of them to go out and chop firewood by day and feed the rest of the people so they would not have to resort to begging.

While the mosque was being built, the Prophet stayed with Abū Ayyūb al-Anṣārī, since he had no house of his own and refused to accept the extravagant gifts his followers were eager to shower him with. He limited himself to accepting some special meals that his neighbors used to send. After the mosque was complete, a few rooms were built next to it for the Prophet and his family. Each room was tiny, only about 135 square feet.

True Brotherhood

The Muslims who migrated assumed the respectful title of "The Emigrants" [al-Muhājirūn], because they abandoned their homeland for the sake of Islam. The Muslims in Madīnah were called "The Helpers" [al-Anṣār] because they helped the former to settle in their new homeland. Many of the people from Makkah had left all their belongings and it was difficult for them to adjust to a foreign environment. There was no doubt that the Muslims of Madīnah would show due hospitality to their penniless Muslims brothers but something of a more enduring nature was needed over mere charity. The Prophet instituted a pact of brotherhood between the two groups by pairing one Emigrant with one Helper. The Helper would share his house and possessions with his Emigrant brother. The people of Makkah were merchants by profession while the people of Madīnah were farmers. When the latter requested that they are willing to give half their land to their Makkan brothers, the Prophet refused. Perhaps he did not want to put too great a burden on the Helpers, or perhaps he knew that they would not be able to take care of the land properly. Instead, it was agreed that the Emigrants would work in the plantations and receive half of the produce.[97] Some of the Makkans began to trade in the local markets and eventually became quite wealthy due to their business acumen. This pact of brotherhood continued for a few years until the Emigrants were able to stand on their own two feet.

---

[97] Bukhārī

Cold War

The Muslims may have escaped the persecution in Makkah, but the Quraysh were still bent on destroying Islam and the Muslims. It was an insult that several members of their own family abandoned their ancestral ways and even fled the city. They were waiting for the right moment to attack the Muslims and finish them off, once and for all. Their first move was to write a threatening letter to ʿAbdullah ibn Ubayy, who was about to be chosen the leader of both the Aws and Khazraj tribes before the Pledge of ʿAqabah.[98] It was only natural that he had some resentment towards the Messenger of Allah since he was given the status and power that would have otherwise belonged to Ibn Ubayy. The letter was clear: "You have given refuge to one of our people. Either kill him, expel him or we will attack you!"[99] The Messenger of Allah found out about the letter and managed to convince Ibn Ubayy that he shouldn't fight his own people. After all, most of Madīnah had already become Muslim and had dedicated themselves to Islam. Ibn Ubayy agreed to the idea, but he continued to openly vent his aversion to Islam.[100]

The situation in Madīnah was dangerous. The Prophet had an armed guard stand outside his door at night due to the severity of the situation.[101] But it was not only the physical threat from Quraysh that made things difficult for the Muslim community but rather the political situation. In Makkah, the Prophet was able to meet with all the tribes of Arabia during the pilgrimage season so that everyone may learn about the message of Islam.

---

[98] Bukhārī
[99] Abu Dawud
[100] Bukhārī
[101] Bukhārī

However, in Madīnah, the Muslims not only lost that opportunity but now the Quraysh utilized their influence in Arabia to block several tribes from even visiting Madīnah. A strategy was needed to reduce the hostility of the Quraysh and perhaps even agree to mutual coexistence.

Now that Madīnah was a city with a new identity, its space and authority had to be recognized by the neighboring communities. A society cannot exist in absolute isolation from its surrounding elements. Since there was no central government in Arabia, tribes and communities related to one another through alliances and treaties. In the absence of either, it meant that they were potentially at war. A tribe would only enter into an agreement if there was some incentive for them. The Quraysh, being the mighty force that they were, had nothing to gain by making a treaty with the Muslims.

The Prophet understood the situation perfectly well but was unable to do anything until the verses were finally revealed: "Those who have been attacked are permitted to take up arms because they have been oppressed– God has the power to give them victory. Those who have been expelled from their homes unjustly, for no other reason besides their statement, 'Allah is our Lord.'"[102] Before this, Muslims were not allowed to fight back at all, even in self-defense. This is why so many Muslims had been tortured and humiliated in Makkah. Now, the permission to fight back was given because the circumstances had changed.

The Prophet immediately adopted a three pronged strategy. He sent out armed expeditions to accomplish three related, but distinct, objectives. One: to gather intelligence about what the

---

[102] Qur'an 22:39-40

Quraysh were up to and to track the movements of their caravans. Two: to conclude peace agreements and enter into alliances with various tribes around Arabia, particularly those on the way to Makkah. Three: to block off and harass the trade caravans of the Quraysh which had to travel in the direction of Madinah in order to get to Syria. The economic blockade would put pressure on the Quraysh to concede to a treaty with the Muslims and would also disrupt their trade which might be used to finance a war against Muslims.

On the Brink of War

The situation continued this way for several months. The Muslims concluded a number of peace treaties with various tribes. Intelligence about Quraysh activities was constantly pouring into Madīnah and their caravans were forced to take inconvenient detours in order to get to Syria. But the Quraysh refused to budge. They had no interest in making peace with the Muslims. There were a few small clashes here and there between the Muslims and Quraysh, but no one was killed.

In the month of Rajab 2 A.H.[103], the Prophet sent ʿAbdullah ibn Jaḥsh to a place called Nakhlah, near Makkah, on an intelligence mission with only 12 armed men. ʿAbdullah saw four noble men from the Quraysh and decided, against the Prophet's orders, to attack them. It was the last day of the month of Rajab, which was one of the four sacred months where Arabs were not allowed to fight. Nonetheless, he attacked, perhaps not realizing that there was still one day left in Rajab. He killed ʿAmr ibn al-Ḥaḍramī and took two prisoners along with their possessions, while one of them managed to escape. ʿAbdullah returned to Madīnah and was rebuked by the Prophet for what he had done. His orders were only to gather intelligence, not to kill anyone or steal anything. The Prophet released the two prisoners and ordered that their wealth be returned. But the damage had already been done and the Quraysh found the excuse they were looking for to attack the Muslims.

The Quraysh immediately began preparations to attack Madīnah. Around the same time, a large trade caravan led by Abu Sufyan was on its way back from Syria. Abu Sufyan was one of the leaders of Quraysh and had fortified his caravan with

---

[103] A.H. means 'after *ḥijrah* [migration]' and is used to date events.

about forty armed soldiers. The Prophet set out from Madīnah with about 300 soldiers in the direction of the caravan. It is uncertain whether or not he knew that the Quraysh were sending an army to attack them, but it is very possible given the number of soldiers that accompanied him. Abu Sufyan immediately headed west, towards the Red Sea to evade the Muslim army. In the meantime, over a thousand soldiers had already been dispatched by the Quraysh. Whether this army intended to attack Madīnah or to simply defend the caravan is uncertain. The only thing that is known for sure is that these two armies would meet, face to face, in the first battle between the Muslims and the Quraysh.

The Battle of Badr

As soon as it was confirmed that the enemy was on its way, the Prophet consulted with his followers whether to pursue the caravan or head back towards Madīnah. Abu Bakr and ʿUmar both spoke up and expressed their willingness to pursue. The Prophet asked the same question again. Another Emigrant answered in the affirmative. The Messenger of Allah asked for the third time whether or not they should return to Madīnah. One of the leaders representing the Helpers understood the Prophet's hesitation and responded, "Do as you please, we are with you. I swear by Allah, if you wanted to cross the sea and were to jump in, we would jump in behind you." This is the confirmation that the Prophet had sought. When the people of Madīnah agreed to protect the Prophet, the agreement was restricted to defending the city only. The Prophet wanted to make sure that the Helpers were willingly agreeing to fight outside the city as well.

The Muslims reached Badr, a small village about 80 miles from Madīnah. Every year a trade fair was hosted in this location, but for now it was abandoned. The Muslims reached Badr first and stopped at a particular location. One of the companions, Hubab ibn al-Mundhir, asked the Prophet, "Are we commanded by Allah to stop here?" The Prophet responded in the negative. Hubab said, "Then I suggest we move forward to the largest well and camp there. That way we can cut off the water supply from the thirsty enemy." The Prophet immediately accepted his wise advice and the army relocated.

Before the Quraysh arrived, there was some discussion about how to proceed. Quite a few people were against the idea of war, the same way they were against the economic boycott of Abū Ṭālib years earlier. There were several reasons for their reluctance. First, many of their own family members had accepted Islam and they did not want to fight them. Second, the caravan of Abu Sufyan had reached the Red Sea and was safe, so there could be no excuse of taking defensive measures. Third, one of the Makkan leaders offered to pay the blood money of ʿAmr ibn al-Ḥadramy who had been killed. This would have been a sufficient expiation according to Arab custom and no revenge would have been necessary. But the loud voices of the warmongers, like Abu Jahl, drowned out the voices of reason and compassion. The Zuhrah clan didn't seem to care what the Quraysh decided and they headed back to Makkah. The clan of Hāshim was also reluctant to fight, but the pressure of Quraysh was too much for them. The Quraysh were still fully armed with over a thousand men, most of them clad in armor, and a hundred horses. Makkah had sent all the leading men of the Quraysh in this army. The Muslims, on the other hand, had only three hundred ill-equipped soldiers and two horses.

Before the battle began, it started to rain. It gave the Muslims an opportunity to clean themselves in the desert while it slowed down the Quraysh who had not yet reached Badr.[104] Furthermore, the Muslim army was overcome by sleep the night before, so they were fresh in the morning. Everyone slept until dawn except the Prophet who stayed awake all night praying to Allah for victory.

The next morning, the two armies were facing each other. It was the month of Ramaḍān, over a year after migrating to Madīnah. The Prophet arranged the ranks of his army and make sure each soldier was in position. The battle began with three duels. Ḥamzah, ʿAlī and ʿUbaydah fought the relatives of ʿAmr

---

[104] Qur'an 8:11

ibn al-Ḥadramī who came forward for vengeance. All three of the Quraysh soldiers fell, while ʿUbaydah was also left fatally injured. Then the battle immediately broke out. Family members were fighting each other, father versus son and brother against brother. The Muslims were physically outnumbered, but with the help of Allah, they managed to overcome the Quraysh army who began to retreat. Seventy idolaters were killed while another seventy were taken prisoner. Most of the leaders of the Quraysh were killed that day, including the notorious Abu Jahl. The Muslims only lost about fourteen men.

Post-war Conduct

The true moral character of a victorious army cannot only be seen in their conduct during war, but after the conflict has ended. The prisoners of war were handcuffed and put under the charge of different Muslim soldiers. The Prophet ordered that they be treated and fed well. Some companions took the words of the Prophet so seriously that they gave their prisoners bread to eat while they settled only for dates themselves.[105] They were even given better clothes to wear than the Muslims wore themselves. After returning to Madinah, ʿUmar recommended that the captives be put to death, since they would probably return to attack the Muslims if they were set free. However, Abu Bakr suggested that they should be ransomed, since many of them were family members and the ransom money could be used for Islam. The Prophet accepted Abu Bakr's advice and the rich prisoners were ransomed while the literate ones had to teach ten Muslims to read and write in order to secure their release.

Meanwhile, in Makkah, the Quraysh were mourning over their dead. With mixed emotions of sadness and anger, they vowed that they would have revenge. The news of the Muslim victory spread like wildfire throughout Arabia and changed the image of Islam. Most Arabs assumed that Islam would be a short-lived phenomenon that would soon die out, but the Battle of Badr had made it clear that the Muslims were a force to be reckoned with. Not only did their respect spread in Arabia but their own self-confidence increased. The Muslims had turned the other cheek for thirteen years and now they would no longer be used as punching bags by the Quraysh.

---

[105] Ṭabarī

New Enemies

It might have appeared that the Prophet and his followers, being hundreds of miles away from Makkah, enjoyed a safer position than they previously were in. However, that is not entirely true. In Makkah, there was only one enemy: the Quraysh. In Madīnah, despite having the strategic advantage of possessing an entire city, two new hostile forces arose, particularly after the Battle of Badr.

The first, and most dangerous of these enemies, came from within. There were still several Arabs in Madīnah who clung to idol worship and detested Islam such as ʿAbdullah ibn Ubayy and his followers. However, after the victory at Badr, most of them professed to be Muslim, at least outwardly. It was clear from their behavior that true faith had not entered their hearts, but they saw a political advantage of pretending to be Muslim. Several verses of the Qur'an were revealed informing the true Muslims of the threat this group of hypocrites posed to the community. However, the Prophet never singled out anyone and taught his followers to judge people by their actions, since only Allah knows their real intentions. Many of these hypocrites secretly conspired with the Quraysh by night, while praying side by side with the Muslims by day.

The second threat came from the Jewish tribes that had lived both inside and around Madīnah for centuries. They used to live in well-built fortresses that had been constructed to protect them from the majority Arab population. The Jews were the closest to the Muslims in the fundamentals of their faith. They only worshipped Allah and believed in all the prophets up to Mūsā [Moses]. The Qur'an respectfully referred to them, along with the Christians, as 'People of the Book', since they possessed a scripture that originated from Allah. Upon arriving in Madīnah, the Prophet had made a treaty with the Jewish tribes to clearly define relations between them and the Muslims. Among the main elements of the agreement were: both the Muslims and Jews were free to practice their own religion, they would mutually support one another in case a foreign enemy attacked and no treaty would be made with the Quraysh against the Muslims.

Some of the Jews even accepted Islam. One of the leading Rabbis of Madīnah, ʿAbdullah ibn Salām by name, believed that the Messenger of Allah was mentioned in the Torah. However, upon his conversion, he was insulted by the members of his own community. Many of the Jews looked down upon the Prophet due to their ancestral pride. They were from the lineage of Isḥāq [Isaac] while Muḥammad was from the lineage of Ismāʿīl [Ishamel]. In all fairness, the pagan Arabs considered themselves above other people as well, but Islam came to remove all man-made notions of superiority. In a way, it could be said that the Jews had issue with the man, rather than the message, while the pagan Arabs had the opposite problem.

But the Prophet continued to teach the Muslims to behave respectfully with them. A revelation later came that Muslims are allowed to eat meat slaughtered by the People of the Book and even intermarry with them.[106] This was a sign of respect for their religious practices whose principles generally originated from Allah. When the funeral procession of a Jewish man passed by the Prophet, he would stand up out of respect.[107] It was expected that the same kind treatment be reciprocated, but it was not to be. Many Jews would pass by the Muslims and

---

[106] Qur'an 5:5
[107] Bukhārī

say, "as-sām ʿalaykum," meaning "death be upon you." It was a twist of the phrase that Muslims used to greet each other, "as-salām ʿalaykum", meaning "peace be upon you." When the Prophet's second wife, ʿĀishah, heard them she would frustratingly respond, "death be on you and may Allah curse you!" But the Prophet taught her to remain calm and simply respond with, "to you too," implying that if they wished peace then they would receive the same, but it they intended an insult then it would be thrown back at them.[108] The hatred of some of them was so intense that they even used to tell the pagan Arabs that their religion is better than Islam, despite the fact that idol worship is one of the greatest sins according to their scriptures.[109]

One particular incident infuriated the Jews more than anything else. While the Prophet was in Makkah, he used to pray in front of the Kaʿbah, but in the direction of Jerusalem to the north. Facing a specific direction during prayer is a symbolic act, since Allah is not bound by any particular space.[110] In Madīnah, the Prophet had to choose either between Jerusalem to the north or Makkah to the south. He was instructed by Allah to pray towards Jerusalem and the Jews were very happy because they used to face the same direction in prayer. It made them feel as if the Muslims were following them. But the reality was that Islam taught them to respect both children of Ibrāhīm [Abraham]. Since one of them built the temple in Jerusalem while the other built the Kaʿbah, both sites were sacred.

However, just before the Battle of Badr, verses were revealed to the Prophet that the Muslims should now face towards Makkah.[111]

---

[108] Bukhārī
[109] Qur'an 4:51
[110] Qur'an 2:177
[111] Qur'an 2:150

This was more than a mere symbolic change. It was clear that Islam was now making a fine line of distinction between itself and the religions of Judaism and Christianity. Islam was not merely a copy, as some might wrongly assume, but a reconnection with the message of Ibrāhīm which had been lost for so many generations. It also made it clear that Makkah was not lost, but rather the Ka'bah would be cleansed of idolatry in the very near future. It strengthened the resolve of the Muslims while upsetting both the Jews and the Quraysh.

Treachery of the Qaynuqā'

A few months after Badr, the Prophet received intelligence that the Jews from the tribe of Qaynuqā', who lived inside Madīnah, were planning to break their covenant. The Prophet had already taken note of their open hostility against Islam, but he had to make sure that the information received was correct. He visited them to see how things were, but they gave him a very cold answer, "Just because you defeated an army of Quraysh doesn't make you anything special. If you were to fight us, you would see what we were really made of." The Prophet was convinced that relations had turned sour and something had to be done. Only a few days later, an incident occurred which added more fuel to the fire. A Muslim lady was shopping in the market of the Qaynuqā, as usual, when some Jews began to harass her. She cried out for help, and a Muslim man arrived at the scene. A fight took place, leaving dead one Jew and one Muslim. As agreed upon, the Prophet should have been consulted in order to resolve the incident according to the principles of peace and justice. But instead, the Qaynuqā' prepared for war, hoping that some of the hypocrites would come to their aid as promised.

The Muslims had to react quickly. They gathered an army and besieged the fortress in which the Qaynuqā' had gathered. The hypocrites broke their promise to the Qaynuqā', just as the latter did with the Muslims. After two weeks without receiving any supplies or outside help, they surrendered. Such treachery was worse than war. According to almost all forms of international law, the fighting men should have been killed. But they pleaded with the Prophet to spare their lives. His kindness got the better of him and he decided to let them live. However, he was no fool. The Qaynuqā' were too dangerous to be left inside the city walls of Madīnah. Their belongings were confiscated and they were kicked out of the city. They took up residence with some other Jewish tribes around the area, but instead of appreciate the Prophet's leniency, their hatred grew even stronger.

The Battle of Uḥud

Immediately after the victory at Badr, Madīnah was on high alert. They knew that the Quraysh would try to attack again, but it was not known when. Since most of the leaders of Quraysh had been killed, Abu Sufyan became the new leader. His initial idea of vengeance was quite childish. He mustered up 200 soldiers and attacked some farms a few miles from Madīnah. He managed to burn some houses and plantations until the Prophet assembled an army and pursued them. They fled back to Makkah, dumping all the food they had brought with them for the journey. The Quraysh believed that they had regained some self-respect as a result of this act, and the Muslims thought that their rage might have been quenched. Perhaps there might be room for a peace agreement.

However, in the month of Shawwāl 3 A.H., the Prophet received intelligence that 3000 soldiers were on their way to attack Madinah. The Quraysh had been preparing for a long time and the profits reaped from their caravans were invested into war. The poets of Makkah had been inciting and rousing people with their propaganda tactics for almost a year. There was little time to prepare. The Prophet assembled an army of 1000 soldiers and consulted his companions on whether to meet the army out in the open or remain in the city and defend. He himself preferred the latter option, as did the suspicious ʿAbdullah ibn Ubayy. However, many of the companions that didn't fight in Badr wanted the honor of being able to fight for the sake of Allah. The Prophet gave in to their zeal and the army set out for Mount Uḥud, about two miles from Madinah, where they could meet the enemy. On the way, ʿAbdullah ibn Ubayy exposed some signs of hypocrisy and decided to abandon the Muslim army. "You didn't accept my advice to stay in the city," he shamelessly told the Prophet. He took 300 of his men back with him, leaving the Muslims with only 700 soldiers. But from the Islamic perspective, this was a good sign that the Muslim army had been purified from hypocritical forces.

When the army arrived at Uḥud, the Prophet surveyed the battlefield. He stationed fifty archers on a nearby hill to guard a small mountain pass that could potentially by exploited by the enemy. The battle began and the Muslims were outnumbered again, but by the help of Allah they began to overcome the Quraysh. The battle-flag of the Quraysh fell and they began to retreat, while the Muslim soldiers continued to pursue them. At that very moment, a mistake occurred which would change victory into defeat. The archers who were positioned on the hill decided to leave their posts. Their leader ordered them to stay where they were, but their eyes were already hypnotized by the spoils of war which they were eager to collect. The spoils left behind by enemy soldiers were like the salary of the army. They were afraid that if they didn't collect it quickly, there would be none left for them.

Khālid ibn al-Walīd, from the Quraysh, was an excellent military strategist. He immediately noticed that the mountain pass was now unprotected and lead his horsemen around the back of the mountain, just as the Prophet had suspected. There were only a few archers left on the mountain and they were taken out pretty quickly by Khālid and his forces. The fleeing soldiers of Quraysh turned around and launched a counter attack. The Muslims were squeezed in from both sides. Most soldiers didn't realize what was happening. Just as they were beginning to make sense of the situation, the Prophet was knocked off his horse and a rumor began to spread that he had been killed.

Some of the companions were on the verge of giving up, when the rumor proved to be false.

"The Prophet is here, he's ok!" someone shouted. Both the Muslims and the idolaters rushed towards him, one intending to defend while the other intending to attack. The companions surrounded him and shielded him from the arrows being fired in his direction. One sword managed to make its way through the shields and hit the Prophet's face, throwing him down on the floor. He lost one of his teeth and two chain links from his armor had sunk into his cheek. Despite the gravity of the situation, the Prophet only said, "Allah, forgive them for their ignorance."[112] Many companions gave up their lives defending the Prophet during this bloody episode. But their lives were not in vain. The Prophet and his companions managed to fend off the onslaught and ascended the peak of a hill where the enemy couldn't reach them. Abu Sufyan made his way to the hill and shouted out, "this is revenge for Badr!"

Seventy Muslims lay dead on the battlefield while only twenty-two Quraysh were killed. Unlike the Muslims, pagan Arabs had little respect for human corpses. The bloodthirsty Makkans mutilated the bodies of the fallen Muslims and their body parts were worn as trophies.[113] The Prophet was particularly grieved by the loss of his uncle Ḥamzah, whose body had been severely disgraced. The corpses were buried and the Muslims headed back towards Madīnah. The Prophet's face continued to ooze out blood until his daughter came and cauterized the wound.[114] The victory at Uḥud had turned into a bitter defeat. Verses were revealed to the Prophet making it clear that the calamity was a

---

[112] Muslim
[113] Bukhārī
[114] Bukhārī

result of the spiritual disease of greed. But the verses also indicated that Allah had forgiven those people, since it was a momentary lapse on their part, rather than an intentional act of disobedience. The Muslims had learned a great lesson: they would not be guaranteed victory unless they acted in accordance with the principles of Islam.

Preachers Murdered

The loss at Uḥud was not only physical but it also marred the reputation of the Muslims. It gave a clear signal to neighboring tribes that the Muslims were indeed vulnerable. The tribes of ʿUḍal and al-Qārah requested the Prophet to send some Muslims to teach them about Islam, so they might consider accepting it. The Messenger of Allah dispatched six knowledgeable Muslims to the region. However, they were ambushed at Rajīʿ on the way by 200 archers. Four of them were killed while the other two were captured and sold to the Quraysh to be tortured and executed.

A few months later, the tribe of ʿĀmir requested the Prophet to send a large group of Muslim teachers to educate the entire tribe about Islam. The Muslims had learned their lesson and were on their guard, but the tribe of ʿĀmir was very powerful and gave their word that they would protect the Muslim teachers. The Prophet sent seventy Muslims, mostly from the people of Ṣuffah, to teach them about Islam. However, it turned out that some of the allies of ʿĀmir were corrupt. They intercepted the unarmed Muslim delegation at a well called Ma'ūnah and killed all of them, except one who managed to escape.

Expulsion of Naḍīr

In al-Rabīʿ al-Awwal 4 A.H., the Messenger of Allah received intelligence that the Jews of Naḍīr were planning to betray the Muslims. The Prophet went to visit them in order to set things right, but they made an attempt on his life. He fled the scene and issued an ultimatum: they had ten days to leave with all their possessions. But they insisted on war and began to make alliances with some Arab leaders. The Prophet, again, had to act fast. A Muslim army was sent to besiege the Naḍīr fortress. After ten days, the Prophet ordered that some of their palm trees, their most valuable possession, be cut down.[115] He knew they were watching and hoped that it would put pressure on them to surrender, seeing that there would be nothing left for them if they continued to put up a fight.

They finally surrendered and tried to negotiate for leniency, as the Qaynuqāʿ had received. However, their treachery was much worse. Not only did they attempt to murder the Prophet but they were even given the opportunity to leave with all their belongings. Furthermore, the Prophet had already witnessed the captives of Badr returning to fight again at Uḥud. But his leniency knew no bounds, and he allowed them to leave with whatever belongings they could carry. They relocated to the heavily fortified city of Khaybar, a few hundred miles to the north. Again, rather than expressing any appreciation, they immediately began to plot against the Muslims from afar.

---

[115] Qur'an 59:5

The Battle of the Trench against the Allies

Huyayy, the chief of the Naḍīr, went to Makkah to incite a final attack against Madinah. He easily managed to convince the Quraysh that it was time for one final assault against the Muslims. Abu Sufyan began to recruit allies from different parts of Arabia. The Quraysh managed to muster up 4000 soldiers themselves with another 6000 soldiers coming from the eastern part of Arabia called Najd. As soon as the Messenger of Allah received the news about the massive army, preparations to defend immediately began.

A decision had to be made whether the 3000 strong Muslim army would go out to meet the enemy or remain within the city. Salmān, who was originally from Persia, suggested a foreign war tactic of building a trench around the unfortified parts of the city to keep the enemy at bay. It was a huge project, but it was made easier by the fact that there was some mountainous terrain surrounding Madinah which cavalry would be unable to cross. The idea was accepted and all the Muslims in the city began to dig. After two weeks of full-time effort, there was a fifteen foot deep trench virtually surrounding the entire city. Before the battle began, the hypocrites made various excuses and abandoned the Muslims.

When the coalition army arrived, they were shocked. The Arabs had never seen such a military strategy in use before. But the Quraysh had their tactics as well. They sent a large part of the army to the north of Madinah so that the Muslims would concentrate their defenses in that region. This would leave the south unguarded where they could attempt to cross the trench. It so happened that the only remaining Jewish tribe in Madinah, the Qurayẓah, lived in the south. Huyyay, who accompanied the allied army, paid them a visit and convinced them to defect from the treaty with the Muslims. When the Prophet heard of this treachery, he sent archers to defend the south but concealed the information from the Muslim army. They were in enough trouble as it was and he didn't want them to lose hope by hearing that their southern defense had been compromised. A few of the Quraysh soldiers managed to jump a narrow part of the trench, but they were killed by the Muslim soldiers on the other side.

The siege lasted for almost a month. It was very cold and windy at night and the allies were almost out of supplies. Some of the groups began to leave and there were rumors of betrayal within enemy ranks. Abu Sufyan finally decided to give up and the allies returned, unsuccessful. With the help of Allah, not only were the Muslims saved from fighting but it was a symbolic victory for them. The tides had turned and Madinah was never to be attacked again.

Dealing with the Traitors of Qurayẓah

The threat was over, but there was no time to rest. The Prophet immediately gathered 3000 soldiers and set out to take care of the traitors from Qurayẓah. The Muslim army surrounded their fortress and cut off all their supplies. They put up a fight for almost a month because they were very well aware of what they had done and knew what fate awaited them. Finally, they gave up and pleaded for mercy. The Prophet had already been lenient with the other two Jewish tribes and it was sending a signal in Arabia that anyone can betray the Muslims and still get off easy. But the crime of Qurayẓah was much greater than that of the Qaynuqā' or the Naḍīr. Their treachery occurred during an attack on Madinah and would have led to the extermination of the entire Muslim community. They were not only guilty of breaking the covenant or of trying to kill one man, but of almost killing the entire Muslim society.

The Prophet decided to be lenient toward them in another way. He allowed them to choose who would determine what should be done with them. Before Islam, the Qurayẓah were allied with the Aws tribe against the Khazraj and other Jewish allies. They decided that a man from Aws should be selected to determine their fate, since they had such cordial relations in the past. The Prophet chose one of the leaders of the Aws, Saʿd ibn Muʿādh to decide the judgment. Saʿd ruled that the fighting men be killed and the women and children be taken as war captives. This verdict was in accordance with Jewish law according to the Torah, and no one contested it.[116] The message to the rest of Arabia was loud and clear: the Muslims may be merciful, but will not be taken advantage of.

---

[116] Deuteronomy 20:12-14

The Treaty of Ḥudaybiyah

In Dhul Qaʿdah 6 A.H. the Prophet set out with 1400 Muslims to visit the Kaʿbah. Such a move may have appeared to be insane, given the circumstances, but he had received a revelation from Allah, in the form of a dream, that he was visiting the Kaʿbah with his head shaved. The group of Muslims, headed by the Prophet, made it clear to everyone that they were on a purely religious mission. It was nothing out of the ordinary. Whenever any other tribe wished to visit Makkah, they would usually go during the sacred months where fighting is prohibited, not carry any special weapons for war and take along animals intended to be sacrificed in Makkah. As soon as the Quraysh found out about this, they faced a dilemma. They could not allow their sworn enemy to enter Makkah, but at the same time they couldn't stop or harm them and risk losing their honor in Arabia.

They decided to send Khālid ibn al-Walīd with 200 horsemen to threaten the unarmed Muslims, but the Prophet evaded the battalion by taking a detour around Makkah. Shortly afterwards, the Muslims reached a plain known as al-Ḥudaybiyah, just outside Makkah. The Prophet dispatched a man to inform the leaders that they did not come to fight but to visit the Ka'bah only. He also indicated that they wished to sign a peace treaty. The Prophet had hoped that after the failed attack on Madinah, they would consider a peace with the Muslims, which would grant their caravans safe passage to Syria as well. A negotiator was sent to convince the Muslims to return home, but they persisted in their right to visit the Kaʿbah. Three more negotiators were sent, one after another, but every time an agreement was made, the Quraysh rejected it. Finally, the Prophet decided to send ʿUthman, who still had many tribal connections in Makkah, to negotiate an agreement with the Quraysh.

Three days passed and there was no word from ʿUthmān. A rumor arose that he had been killed, which meant a clear and open declaration to prepare for battle. The Prophet acted quickly, calling all his companions around him. They did not come prepared for war, so they had no armor or shields, but it was customary to carry swords and arrows while travelling through the desert. The Prophet sat under a tree while every companion, both male and female, pledged that they would support the Prophet to the death. This pledge became known later as 'The Pledge of Riḍwān [Satisfaction]' since Allah revealed that he was pleased with those who undertook such an oath.[117] However, soon after, the rumor proved to be false and ʿUthmān returned.

That was not the only good news but a man named Suhayl ibn ʿAmr was sent by the Quraysh to negotiate. He was a very important and clever man, and it was clear that the Makkans were finally willing to compromise. The determination of the Muslims had pressured them to opt for peace. Sharp and heated discussions between the Prophet and Suhayl continued for a long time until the agreement was finally written down and agreed upon. The treaty contained the following provisions:

1. The Muslims and Quraysh would not fight each other for a period of ten years.
2. The Muslims would return to Madīnah and not be allowed to visit the Ka'bah this year. However, they would be allowed to visit the Ka'bah next year for three days only.

---

[117] Qur'an 48:18

3. If any Muslim from Madinah decided to leave Islam and return to Makkah, they would be allowed to do so. However, if anyone from Makkah decided to accept Islam and go to Madinah, he would be returned to the Quraysh.
4. Both parties could make alliances with any tribes they wished, and they would also be bound by the treaty.

When the companions found out about the agreement, they saw it as a slap in the face. Not only was their pilgrimage delayed and severely restricted the following year but an unfair agreement to return any persecuted Muslims back to Makkah was agreed to. Only moments ago, they agreed to fight to the death, and now they were insulted with a one-sided agreement. But the Prophet did not consult them this time, as he normally did. The agreement was a command from Allah, and there is no room for anyone's opinion in such matters.

Islam Spreads

As soon as the Muslims departed, the Prophet received a new revelation, "Indeed, we have opened up a path to clear victory for you," referring to the newly signed peace treaty. After so many years of persecution and warfare, there was finally peace. Muslims and idolatrous Arabs began to interact freely and regularly meet each other. Within the next two years, more people would accept Islam than in the past eighteen years. An environment of pressure and hostility prevents people from thinking clearly. Shortly afterwards, even the staunchest enemies of Islam, like Khālid, who was responsible for the slaughter at Uḥud, and ʿAmr ibn al-ʿĀṣ, who attempted to extradite the Muslims from Abyssinia, opened their hearts towards the message of Islam.

The following year, the Messenger of Allah sent envoys with letters addressed to the leaders of all the major powers in and around Arabia. Most of the letters were similar: they began in the name of Allah, declared that Muhammad is the Messenger of Allah, invited the leaders to accept Islam and warned them that if they rejected they would have to bear the responsibility of preventing the message from reaching their followers. The king of Abyssinia and the king of Baḥrayn accepted Islam while Kisrā, the emperor of Persia, angrily tore the letter to pieces and killed the Muslim envoy. The ruler of northern Arabia also responded with hostility and threatened to attack Madinah. The king of Egypt, Muqawqas, politely declined to accept Islam but sent gifts to the Prophet as a gesture of good will. The Prophet accepted such gifts and maintained friendly relations with him.

When Heraclius, the emperor of Byzantium, received the letter, he began to investigate the issue. He ordered his guards to fetch any Arabs that happened to be in the region so he could ask them some questions. It so happened that no other than Abu Sufyan was in the area on a business venture. He was summoned into the Roman court and his followers were made to stand behind him. Heraclius told him that he would ask him a number of questions about this man who claims to be a prophet and his followers would gesture from behind if he was telling a lie. It was a genius tactic to both ascertain the truth and give the witnesses the safety of contradicting their leader.

The questioning began:

> Heraclius: "What is the status of his lineage amongst you?"
>
> Abu Sufyan: "He has a noble lineage."
>
> Heraclius: "Has anyone prior to him made such a claim before?"
>
> Abu Sufyan: "No."
>
> Heraclius: "Were any of his ancestors a king?"
>
> Abu Sufyan: "No."
>
> Heraclius: "Do the noble people follow him or the weak and poor ones?"
>
> Abu Sufyan: "The weak and poor."
>
> Heraclius: "Are his followers increasing or decreasing?"
>
> Abu Sufyan: "They are increasing."
>
> Heraclius: "Are people leaving his religion out of dislike after entering into it?"
>
> Abu Sufyan: "No."
>
> Heraclius: "Did you ever accuse him of lying before he made this claim?"
>
> Abu Sufyan: "No."
>
> Heraclius: "Has he ever deceived you?"

Abu Sufyan: "*No, but we have a peace treaty right now and we don't know how he might act.*"[118]

Heraclius: "*What does he command you to do?*"

Abu Sufyan: "*He wants us to only worship Allah and abandon idolatry. He wants us to abandon the ways of our ancestors, pray, give charity, etc.*"

Heraclius responded, "I have asked you all these questions to determine whether he is a true prophet. Prophets always appear from the noble families among their people. If someone before him had made the same claim, I could say that he might be imitating them. If one of his ancestors was a king, I could say that he might be trying to restore his kingdom. Since you told me that he was never accused of lying, I wonder why he would refrain from lying to people but then lie about God. You told me that the poor and weak follow him, and that is the case with most prophets of God." He continued explaining the reason behind each question until it became clear to everyone in the royal court that he was inclined towards Islam. The dignitaries, who were Christian, began shouting and yelling. When he realized that his people would never accept Islam, he quieted them down and said, "I was only testing you to see how loyal you are to me." The people calmed down and prostrated themselves in front of him, as was customary. It is unknown what was really in his heart and what happened after that.

---

[118] Abu Sufyan later admitted that this was the only negative statement he was able to slip in during that interrogation.

The Siege of Khaybar

There was relative peace in Arabia, particularly between the Muslims, the Quraysh and all the other tribes who entered into alliances with either one of them. However, there was one major enemy left to the north of Madinah that had no intention in allying with the Muslims, or even now with the Quraysh for that matter. The Jews of Khaybar were heavily influenced by the members of the Qaynuqā' and Naḍīr who blamed the Prophet for their expulsion from Madinah. They were far from being a neutral party. In fact, it is from Khaybar that the Quraysh were incited to amass allied forces and attack Madinah only two years ago. The Prophet received intelligence that they were plotting against the Muslims, so he decided to put an end to the danger before the situation became worse.

Khaybar consisted of several heavily fortified buildings and had the ability to muster up over 10,000 soldiers with the help of their allies. The Prophet decided to take them by surprise in Muḥarram 7 A.H. The Muslim army consisted of only 1600 soldiers who traveled by night and surrounded some of their fortresses. When they awoke in the morning, they realized that their communications had already been cut off and their supplies blocked. This was a perfect opportunity to draft a treaty of peace, but they insisted on war. The Muslims concentrated on one fort at a time, beginning with the weakest first. Fort after fort began to surrender to the siege. The last fort was the most difficult to break and its siege alone lasted two weeks. They finally surrendered on the condition that they would not be killed. After they were defeated, they attempted to bargain with the Prophet. He eventually allowed them to stay in Khaybar since it was a very fertile land and they were experts in taking care of it, but in exchange for a crop tax that they had to pay to the Muslims. This siege concluded all hostilities between the Jews and Muslims.

The Expedition of Mu'tah

A few months later, a group of Muslims traveling towards Syria were murdered by the Ghassān tribe, who were allied with the Romans. The Prophet had to respond, so he sent 3000 soldiers led by Zayd ibn Thābit. He knew that this was near Roman territory and was fully aware of the massive forces that the Romans had at their disposal. Therefore, he announced that if Zayd died, Jaʿfar would be put in charge and, if he was killed, ʿAbdullah ibn Rawāḥah would take over. The Arab tribes banded together and were reinforced by the Byzantine imperial troops. Their army numbered over a hundred thousand fully equipped soldiers.

The Muslims had never seen such a large army before in their life. They consulted one another on whether they should send a message to the Prophet about the size of the army. However, it was decided that they should proceed as planned and not be afraid of the odds. The fighting began and all three leaders were killed. Afterwards, the Muslims appointed Khālid ibn al-Walīd to take charge of the army. He rearranged the army in such a way that they were able to retreat without much further loss of life. When they reached Madinah, the Prophet was very sad that his own adopted son and cousin had been killed. But the Prophet was very proud of Khālid's genius strategy and nicknamed him 'the sword of Allah'.

The Conquest of Makkah

In 8 A.H., the tribe of Bakr attacked the Khuzāʿah tribe who was allied with the Muslims. The Khuzāʿah immediately asked the Prophet for help, since the Bakr were allied with the Quraysh. This was a violation of the treaty of Ḥudaybiyah, and it later turned out that the Quraysh had supplied their ally with weapons to launch the attack. The Quraysh knew they were guilty so they sent Abu Sufyan to Madinah to try and renegotiate a treaty. The Prophet was a man of his word and needed to help his allies, so he remained silent and said nothing in response. The Quraysh were unclear as to what this was supposed to mean. Was the treaty still in effect or broken?

A few weeks later, the Prophet issued orders for several armies to begin marching towards different locations, fully armed. Rumors were circulated that perhaps he was headed to fight the Romans again, or maybe he was headed east to avenge the Muslim preachers that had been murdered. Within a few days, the various armies received instructions that they were to head straight for Makkah and surround it from all sides. Makkah woke up one morning to find itself completely surrounded by a massive Muslim army. The tactic was to startle the Quraysh and frighten them into surrendering peacefully without putting up any fight. Abu Sufyan, viewing the situation and being fully aware of the dedication of the Muslims, decided to give up.

The Messenger of Allah entered Makkah with the massive army and headed straight for the Kaʿbah. He announced to the leaders who had fought him, persecuted his followers and attempted to kill him on several occasions, "Today, you are all free to go. I will not take revenge on you." Upon witnessing the leniency of the Prophet, many Makkans embraced Islam. Then he entered the Kaʿbah and had each and every single idol removed and destroyed. Bilāl ascended the structure and made the call to prayer from the roof of the Kaʿbah. Centuries had passed since the building constructed by Ibrāhīm and his son had been dedicated solely to worshiping Allah alone.

The Battles of Ḥunayn and Ṭā'if

After the defeat of the Quraysh, Arabia was no longer the same. The Muslims were seen as one of the most powerful forces in the entire region. Some tribes saw this as their last opportunity to strike the Muslims before they took over the entire peninsula. The tribe of Ḥawāzin rallied together their allies to wage war on the Prophet. They marched out with a strong army and encamped in the valley of Ḥunayn, a few miles east of Makkah, with their archers strategically positioned on the hills. The Prophet set out with 12,000 Muslims to intercept them. This was the largest and most well-equipped army the Muslims had ever amassed, and there seemed to be some signs of pride in the army ranks. As they entered the valley, they were taken by surprise and showered with arrows from all sides. The narrowness of the valley squeezed them in and many of the Muslim soldiers began to disperse in all directions. Among the few standing firm was the Prophet, who maintained his ground. Eventually, he was able to rally his troops again and launch a counterattack. Within a short span of time, the tides had turned and the enemy was in retreat.

They fled to al-Ṭā'if, where the Prophet had been kicked out and humiliated only a decade ago. The Muslims pursued and launched a siege on the heavily fortified city. After two long weeks of fighting, it was clear that the leaders of the city had enough supplies to last them the entire year, so the Muslim army let them be. The Ḥawāzin had already been defeated and they posed no major threat anymore.

After the Battle of Ḥunayn, the Muslim army had spoils of war like they had never seen in their lives. There were thousands of prisoners and tens of thousands of camels and sheep left by the army who foolishly brought all their possessions to the battlefield. When the time came to distribute the wealth, the Prophet began by giving large amounts to the new Muslims who had only accepted Islam after the conquest of Makkah. Leaders like Abu Sufyan and his family were given hundreds of camels and sheep, and received even more when they demanded a larger share. When the Helpers, who had no direct family relations with the people of Makkah, heard about this unequal distribution, they began to complain. The Prophet gathered them and explained, "I give to one group of people while another group is dearer to my heart. Are you not satisfied that I will return to Madīnah and reside permanently with you?" The Helpers, after brief reflection, got the point immediately. These new Muslims were only being favored because their faith was weak, unlike the Helpers who had no such weakness, and therefore did not require any monetary favoritism. The Prophet returned with his Companions to Madīnah near the end of the 8th year A.H.

The Expedition of Tabūk

In Rajab of the 9th year A.H., the Muslims received intelligence that the Romans were preparing to attack Madīnah. Arabia was never really seen as any threat to either the Persians or the Romans since the Arabs had never been united before. The Prophet, despite the hot summer and famine, decided to go out and meet them before they could enter Arabia. It was one of the most difficult missions since the journey was long, the summer heat was intense, and the Roman forces were among the most disciplined and well-equipped in the world. The Prophet asked everyone to donate whatever they could for the cause. People like Abū Bakr gave away all their wealth, while the more wealthy Muslims donated large sums of money and supplies. Despite all the generosity, there were many people who could not afford to join the army and returned home with tears in their eyes.[119] Thirty thousand companions set out with the Prophet towards the north. When they reached Tabūk in Northern Arabia, the Romans were nowhere to be found. It seems that they were scared off by the approaching Muslim army, but the Prophet camped there for twenty days just in case they might consider an attack. The sheer size of the Muslim army sent a message throughout both Arabia and the Byzantine Empire: the Muslims were a force to be reckoned with. Several tribes in the north got the message and realized that they would no longer need to ally with the Romans to guarantee their security, so they drafted peace treaties with the Prophet.

When the Muslim army returned to Madīnah, there were accounts to be settled. The Prophet had made it very clear that all able-bodied Muslims are required to march out on this expedition, despite the hardships involved. The only ones who

---
[119] Qur'an 9:92

were exempted from such duty were the old and the ill. Yet, there were several people who remained behind, and they came to the Prophet making various excuses. It didn't take a genius to figure out that these were the hypocrites who stayed behind, but the Prophet accepted their excuses, at least outwardly. There were three Muslims, however, who openly admitted that they had no excuse but their own laziness. The Prophet instituted a fifty day long social boycott on these three. No Muslim was to speak to them or communicate with them in any way. Since these were true believers, the most difficult thing for them was being unable to communicate with the Prophet himself. After fifty days, a revelation came down that Allah had forgiven them. They were extremely thankful and had learned their lesson.

After the conquest of Makkah and the Expedition of Tabūk, dozens of Arab tribes throughout the entire peninsula began sending delegations to Madīnah in order to officially declare their acceptance of Islam. Most of the Arabs had taken a wait-and-see attitude to the conflict between the Muslims and Quraysh. Many of them had an intrinsic belief that if Muhammad was indeed a true prophet then Allah would give him victory. Now it was clear to them that the Muslims were indeed victorious, so they pledged their loyalty. However, not all of these tribes were sincere in their beliefs. Verses were revealed about the reality of some people who professed Islam only with their tongues:

> *The desert Arabs say, "We have believed." Tell them, "You have not believed. Rather, you should say: 'We have submitted.' Faith has not yet entered your hearts."*[20]

---

[120] Qur'an 49:14

The Qur'an made it clear that someone may acquire certain benefits in this world by entering the fold of Islam outwardly, but will only really benefit from it when they enter wholeheartedly. There were other tribes who visited the Prophet and concluded a treaty of peace, since they were not interested in accepting Islam.

The Farewell Pilgrimage

Near the end of 9 A.H., the Prophet informed the tribes around Arabia that he was planning to personally perform pilgrimage to Makkah. About a hundred thousand Muslims from all over Arabia took up the opportunity to be with the Prophet and made their way to Makkah. Undertaking the journey was a clear demonstration of their newfound faith in Islam, since there were no idols left in Makkah. While performing the rituals associated with the Pilgrimage, the Prophet stood on a mountain in the plains of ʿArafāt and delivered a speech to an audience of about 150,000 Muslims, known as the 'farewell sermon'. The lecture consisted of the following revolutionary points:

- All sums of interest on loans are cancelled
- All tribal retaliation for past murders are cancelled
- Women have rights over men, who must be careful to fulfill those rights
- The blood and property of a Muslim is sacred, so no one should violate that sanctity unjustly
- No Arab has any superiority over a non-Arab, or vice versa. The color of your skin does not determine superiority.

The Prophet's Death

The Prophet's mission was complete. He had conveyed the message of Islam and uprooted the idolatry and social vices from the entire Arabian Peninsula. About two months after returning from Makkah, the Messenger of Allah was hit with a high fever and headache. He became very weak, but continued to go to the mosque and lead the prayers sitting down, while the rest of the Muslims stood behind him. Finally, after a few days, he was too ill to even get up to go to the mosque. Every time he washed himself and tried to get up, he fainted. Therefore, upon waking up again, he signaled that Abu Bakr should lead the people in prayer, while he prayed in his room. This continued for several days until he finally passed away in the morning on the 12th of al-Rabī' al-Awwal.

When the Muslims, who were waiting inside the mosque, heard what had happened, they were stunned. 'Umar pulled out his sword and yelled, "Anyone who says the Prophet is dead, I'll chop his head off right now!" Perhaps he assumed that the hypocrites were spreading lies, or maybe he was so overwhelmed with grief that he was in a state of denial. Abu Bakr walked into the room where the Prophet lay, verified the information, and came out to let the people know that it was the truth. But people were so emotional they were not paying attention. So Abu Bakr stood in one corner of the mosque, raised his voice, and began to speak: "People, listen up! Whoever worshipped Muhammad should know that he is now dead! But whoever worshipped Allah, know that He is alive and will never die!" Then he recited a verse from the Qur'an, which everyone was familiar with, but had eluded them through their heightened emotions:

> *Muhammad is only a messenger before whom many messengers have come and gone. If he dies or is killed, would you revert to your old ways? If anyone did so, he would not harm Allah in the least. Allah will reward the grateful.*[121]

The Muslims immediately came to their senses. It was as if this verse was just revealed for the first time. The message was crystal clear: the Prophet was only a vehicle through which the message of Allah was to be delivered. The success of any human being lies in connecting with the Teacher of the teacher, and following the guidance of Allah.

---

[121] Qur'an 3:144

Epilogue

Both friend and foe have had to, willingly or unwillingly, admit that Muhammad was the most successful of all religious personalities in the history of the world. A thorough inspection of history cannot reveal any other reformer who brought about such a complete transformation of society in such a little time, and with so little means at his disposal. Hundreds of evils, both spiritual and moral, from prostitution to drinking and gambling were entirely uprooted from a society addicted to these vices.

Those who walk away from the story of Muhammad with an admiration for the character and determination of the Prophet are entitled to such a view. Many people would admire that he was a kind hearted man, a skillful military commander, a simple man unconcerned with things of this world, etc. Everyone sees the world through their own lenses, and they appreciate and admire certain characteristics in a person that are relevant and meaningful to them. However, to limit yourself to seeing what you want to see, especially in a man who claimed to be the last link between God and man, is like that of a person traveling down a dangerous path. He meets a man on the way who warns him about the impending dangers that lie ahead, but instead of focusing on the advice or trying to determine whether the man is honest, he begins to admire his clothes and is amused by the man's accent. Muhammad preached a message and warned about the dangers of not following that guidance. Justice would require that his claim to prophethood be at least given *some* due consideration by those who have been presented with the message of Islam.

Appendix 1 – Early Sources

The earliest extant works of Sīrah are those by Ibn Isḥāq [d. 151 AH], al-Wāqidī [d. 207 AH], Ibn Saʿd [d. 230 AH], and al-Ṭabarī [d. 310 AH]. Most scholars who came after them relied almost entirely on these books. The work of Ibn Isḥāq, which was later summarized by Ibn Hishām, was intended for mass consumption and is the book which popularized the subject. It remains the most widely used book on the subject and is mistakenly considered to be the most authoritative due to its popularity. However, other scholars such as al-Zarqānī, Ibn Ḥajar, al-Dhahabī, and Ibn Kathīr opted for a different method of studying the *sīrah*. They attempted to combine the Ḥadīth reports with these biographical books and give preference to the former whenever there was a conflict since the field of Ḥadīth is a more precise and authentic science. Such an endeavor required expertise in both fields which was a rare asset. Any attempt to research something about the life of the Prophet must refer to the following materials: the Qur'an, Ḥadīth, biographies of the Prophet, biographies of the companions, and general history books.

Printed in Poland
by Amazon Fulfillment
Poland Sp. z o.o., Wrocław